# PAINTING
# ON
# PORCELAIN

# Dony Karandjoulov-Alexiev

# Painting on Porcelain

## In the Oriental Style

Photographs : Jean-Marc Lalier and Joel Bloquet

Translation: John Gilbert

Studio
Vista

## ACKNOWLEDGEMENTS

*The author thanks the ADAC for placing their workshops at his disposal for the purpose of taking photographs*

Cassell Publishers Limited
Villiers House, 41/47 Strand
London WC2N 5JE

English translation by John Gilbert

First published in Great Britain 1994
by arrangement with
Armand Colin Éditeur
103 Boulevard Saint-Michel
75240 Paris Cedex 05

British Library Cataloguing in Publication Data
A catalogue record for this book is available from the British Library

ISBN 0 289 80128 1

Distributed in the United States by Sterling Publishing Co. Inc.
387 Park Avenue South, New York, New York 10016-8810

Distributed in Australia by Capricorn Link (Australia) Pty Ltd
2/13 Carrington Road, Castle Hill, NSW 2154

Typeset by Blackjacks Ltd, London
Printed and bound in Italy by E.B.S.

# Contents

# *Introduction*

*The master says: think deeply about what is known,*
*learn what is new and never stop teaching...*
Analects of Confucius

The fir, the bamboo and the prunus in combination form a motif that recurs frequently. Highly decorative, it is also charged with meaning. It stands, for example, for the 'Three Friends', symbolising Confucius, Buddha and Lao-Tzu.

The story goes that on one occasion each man tasted from a jar of vinegar placed before them. Lao-Tzu pronounced that it tasted pleasant. Buddha considered it to taste bitter. Confucius declared it to be acidic. Yet all agreed that it was the same liquid. This legend demonstrates that the three systems of thought draw their inspiration from the same source

I began this book with high expectation and ended up regretting not having included everything I would have liked. But there was so much of interest to describe and to illustrate that I soon came to realise that no single book could possibly contain it all.

In any work devoted to the practice of an art, it is not enough simply to learn techniques and to imagine that progress depends on using those methods that take up the least time. We have to understand how that art originated and developed, to place it in historical context and to examine its centuries of achievement.

The art of ceramics is one of the earliest to have been practised, motivated by man's basic need for vessels and containers. The first craftsmen conceived the idea of mixing earth and water, of hollowing out this paste and of drying it in the sun. When they learned how to make fire, they hardened their hand-modelled pottery pieces by exposing them to heat. Having taken this revolutionary step, impelled by native ingenuity and aesthetic instinct, subsequent generations improved upon these primitive creations, sometimes producing incomparable masterpieces. Only by going back in history can we appreciate the cultural wealth created and accumulated by our ancestors – wealth that is part of our inheritance. Any such journey cannot fail to be a rich source of ideas and inspiration.

Study of the past reveals that creative minds have invariably drawn from a common crucible, copying and adapting until they have attained newer and ever higher levels of achievement. It might be expected that individual civilisations, far removed from one another in time and space, would tend to diverge as they retreated

back to their origins; yet, despite the immense geographical distances involved, there have been continual cross-influences. Exchanges in trade and communications between the great civilisations of Asia and Europe, albeit occasionally tenuous and discontinuous, have existed since prehistoric times.

The historical section of this book aims to describe the art of ceramics of the Far East and the influence it exerted upon Europe. The subject is so vast that it is only possible to give an overview. If it fuels the desire to explore the topic further and in more detail, that aim will have been attained.

The other objective of the book is to provide a selection of accessible models for decoration in the Oriental style, and to explain, step by step, how to go about creating simplified but aesthetically pleasing versions of these models. The choice of original subjects has been difficult. For each one illustrated, there are a dozen others, just as beautiful, that had to be omitted. Here again there is ample scope for branching out in different directions.

The book is divided broadly into three parts. The first deals with the ceramics of the Far and Middle East; and, because a civilisation's art cannot possibly be dissociated from its history, this is accompanied by an outline history of China, Japan and the Islamic world. Information about civilisations other than our own is all the more important today now that rapid locomotion and communication have combined to make our world seem strangely small. And since we live in societies that are increasingly cosmopolitan it is surely worth deepening mutual

understanding by finding out all we can about other people and their cultures.

The second part shows the influence that these civilisations have had at various intervals upon the West, most particularly in the field of ceramics. The subjects chosen are designed to show how the Europeans, after copying the arts of the Far East, arrived at original creations in which the native exotic element lost its character and gradually disappeared. Take an example still very close to us: in the nineteenth century, the impact of Japan upon European art was enormous. This influence was thoroughly absorbed in the production of genuinely European works: Japanism was transformed into Art Nouveau.

It is not entirely correct to speak of reciprocal cultural influence solely as a feature of the past. The fact is that we are still fascinated by the arts of the Orient. The martial arts, yoga, acupuncture and the like have become familiar and are widely practised in the West; courses on Chinese and Japanese painting and calligraphy are on the increase. As far as porcelain is concerned, it is sufficient to take a look at industrial production over the last few decades to see that Oriental motifs are continuously in demand; when they are not reproduced in the classic manner, they are the source of models.

The third part of the book assembles all the technical advice that may be helpful in realising the models suggested in the previous sections. Sometimes the explanations are lengthy but this is merely in the interests of clarity, to provide complete information.

# CHINA:
# BLUE-AND-WHITE

# History of China

It is very difficult to establish the date when ceramics appeared in China. Funeral vases that have come to light in excavations testify to the fact that pottery existed from the early Neolithic Age. Already there was a very simple concept of decoration, restricted to geometrical forms, either painted in red-and-black (*caitao*) or engraved.

This was the departure point of a long and laborious technical evolution in the quest for forms, glazes and designs. It was to culminate in the marvellous porcelain products of China that would fascinate the Western world. It is important to emphasise that developments in the processes of firing were determining factors in the onward march of Chinese civilisation and, consequently, in the evolution of ceramics. The capacity to fire at high temperatures was essential for metal-working and enabled China to enter the Bronze Age. But progress in this field was of equal benefit to the manufacture of ceramics. Thus there are pieces of shard pottery, rendered extremely hard under conditions of great heat, dating from the third millennium BC.

Fired at temperatures of 1300°–1400°C, feldspar, present in clay, would vitrify to form a natural glaze on the surface of these pieces, giving them brilliance and impermeability. One form of clay employed was kaolin, the crucial element of porcelain. These wares date from the Shang dynasty (1766–1122BC) and are known as protoporcelain. The arts of bronze and ceramics were for a long time closely allied. Bronze objects inspired pottery from the very start, and over the centuries their elegant shapes and decorative motifs served as models for ceramics in a multitude of forms.

Specialists describing the history of ceramics from this period use the names of successive ruling dynasties, which mark fairly accurately the different phases through which they progressed. Without going into great detail, it is useful to know the principal landmarks and brief outlines of the long history of China.

The Qin dynasty (221–206BC) unified China and built the Great Wall in the north of the country to protect it against invasions by barbarian tribes. Large-scale enterprises indicate that this period was marked by important inventions and technical advances. The 'First Emperor', Qin Shihuang, introduced far-reaching reforms for the later development of the country.

He was buried together with the symbolic representation of his army in terracotta, comprising 600 statues of horses and 7000 statues of warriors, each of them different. The emperor had this sepulchre prepared during his lifetime and the statues were made from casts of real members of his guard. He thus broke with the cruel ancient tradition of human sacrifice, which decreed that dead monarchs should be accompanied in their departure for the afterlife.

The Han dynasty (206BC–AD220) organised and built the Chinese state, which saw the nation emerge as a military power, extending its rule to Manchuria, to Korea, to Tonkin and its outposts, and as far as Transoxiana and Fergana (Turkestan). This was the first great Chinese empire. Power was centralised, with a civil service consisting of scholar-functionaries brought up in public or private schools and recruited by examination. The official doctrine was Confucianism.

It was also a period of peace, auspicious for the development of the arts. The Han monarchs were builders. Architects built palaces and temples, their walls covered with frescos. The appearance of these vanished paintings can be imagined thanks to scenes engraved on the brick and stone, as well as by written texts.

Ceramic bricks, tiles and acroteria (pedestals for ornaments) formed part of this architectural endeavour. Lead glaze, probably brought from the Middle East, was adopted and, more importantly, one of the two branches of Chinese ceramics made its appearance: the grey-green Yue products, ancestors of the famous celadons. Much of this ceramic production was designed for funerary rituals, which consisted in surrounding the dead person with all that he or she needed in the afterlife. 'Substitutes' (*ming-k'i*) represented houses and its occupants. Thanks to these ceramic statuettes, the dead individual was accompanied by domestic animals, by musicians and dancers, by elegant ladies and servants. They provide an interesting glimpse into living conditions at the time.

The Han emperors also promoted the export of Chinese art. The Great Wall was not strong enough to keep out the powerful nomadic peoples; nor were they halted by temporary treaties or impressive gifts offered as tribute in exchange for peace. Under this foreign threat, the Chinese were obliged to seek alliances with neighbouring kingdoms in the south or to win their submission. These diplomatic missions and military expeditions engaged in exchanges of goods, which introduced Chinese products abroad. By virtue of barter and commerce, some products, including silk, reached the West. Drawing to its close, the Han dynasty was shaken by revolts. Successive waves of barbarians invaded northern China.

**The North and South dynasties** The collapse of the Han dynasty was followed by the break-up of their kingdom. The north came under foreign domination, the south saw several dynasties following one another.

The conquerors quickly assimilated Chinese culture and embraced Buddhism, which had been introduced to China in the Han period. The expansion of Buddhist art brought a wide diversity of subjects to painting, and this was also reflected in the decoration of ceramics.

The application of high-fire processes was decisive for the evolution of ceramics. Mastery of the techniques of firing led to the perfecting of glazes. Towards the end of the fifth century, forms were very refined with decorative elements engraved or cut in relief. The end of this period saw the appearance of light grey, close-grained stoneware, with increasingly hard glazes.

Chinese warriors
Design by N. Caramanis

■ Elongated blue dragon

It was not until the great T'ang dynasty (AD618–906) that China was reunified, endowed with a well organised and prosperous administration. It rapidly extended its rule over Korea, northern Indochina and Sinkiang. The frontiers were well protected and caravans travelled its territories in safety. The capital of Ch'ang-an, present-day Xi'an, was a cosmopolitan centre of culture and commerce. Foreigners converged by land and by sea, bringing with them the produce of distant countries as well as their ideas, techniques and arts. Peace, and the wealth of this cosmopolitan civilisation, contributed to the blossoming of the arts of calligraphy, poetry, music and painting. The renown of T'ang China, with its unprecedented power and brilliant culture, spread across eastern Asia. Through the intermediary of Arab merchants, who held the trade monopoly with the West, it extended to the rest of the known world. Certain inventions, notably those of paper and porcelain, played a vital role in this diffusion.

In the second half of the ninth century during the T'ang dynasty a fine, translucent white porcelain was produced, rendered shiny and waterproof by a feldspar glaze. The discovery of this white porcelain occurred a full seven hundred and fifty years before the appearance, at Meissen, of the first European prototypes.

The makers of ceramics also adopted new oxides as colorants, notably oxides of copper, manganese and cobalt, and their use determined the 'three colours' style. In both form and decoration the influence of the Islamic Middle East was evident.

The production of funerary figurines continued, reflecting daily life and beliefs. It constituted an astonishing portrait gallery which brought to life a crowd of dignitaries, ladies and dancers, knights and camel-drivers, servants and merchants, and foreigners from many parts, all of whom thronged the streets of Ch'ang-an. The use of *ming-k'i* would disappear under the ensuing dynasties with changes in funeral rites.

■ Two phoenixes. The background, in the interstices, should be filled for preference with flower sprigs or a decorative motif
In China the dragon was the emblem of the emperor and the phoenix that of the empress

Towards the end of the ninth century the signs of decline were followed by discontent and disorder. China sank into anarchy and went through a tragic period which led to the fall of the T'ang dynasty.

**The Five Dynasties** (AD907–960) General disorder provoked the disintegration of the country and in less than a century five dynasties succeeded one another, giving their name to the period. Times were hard but such difficulties proved stimulating for artistic creation, which continued to develop in the great T'ang tradition.

It was at this period that the celadons produced at Yüeh attained perfection: their elegance of form was highlighted by a brilliant, mellow glaze. Scholars of the age compared the whiteness of their porcelain tea-bowls to silver. Decoration was often incised, representing phoenixes, dragons and flowers. Chinese texts reveal that 'secret' or 'reserved' porcelain for the use of the sovereigns was manufactured to order in the kilns of Yu-hsien.

This period ended with the accession of the Song in AD960.

The rule of the **Song dynasty (AD960–1279)** was distinguished by two periods. The first, the Northern Song, was marked by a policy of reorganisation and reform with a view to strengthening the country's power. These were energetic emperors, not dedicated to war, who preferred to buy peace rather than attempt to contain the pressure of the Mongol tribes. In 1126 northern China was invaded by the Jurchen Tartars. The Song did not endeavour to regain the lost territories and their capital was transferred. The second, the Southern Song period, was of short duration and ended with the invasion of the Mongols in 1279.

These emperors, great aesthetes, patrons and often artists themselves, focused their interest mainly on arts and culture. The visual arts, literature and Chinese civilisation as a whole attained levels of extreme refinement and brilliance. Active commercial links were once more resumed, although the Silk Road, which had become dangerous because of the Mongol invasions, was abandoned. Trade was conducted mainly by sea, and above all by the Arabs. Chinese products, including celadons and porcelains, were increasingly in vogue and prized particularly in Japan and the Middle East.

This favourable climate gave a great impetus to the manufacture of porcelain and numerous workshops sprang up in southern China. Production was very varied and decoration was inspired by painting on silk and paper. Especially noteworthy was the appearance of blue-and-white porcelain, which was to enjoy a glorious future.

However, the Song ceramics that were considered the most perfect were those in which sobriety almost reached austerity: these simple, pure forms and subtle colours remained unequalled. The *yue* of the Song era were universally known. They arrived in Europe in the fourteenth century and the name celadon was later given to them in France. It derived from the green ribbons of the shepherd Celadon, hero of the famous seventeenth-century novel *Astrée*, by Honoré Urfé.

On the cultural plane there was excitement in the philosophical and intellectual fields. It produced many important works as well as the tradition of scholar–painters. These scholars aimed to give another dimension to painting by adding poetic texts or philosophic reflections, using the art of calligraphy. Their style, less formal and precise, became very personal and expressive – not far removed from Impressionism.

Commercial activity was highly organised. Trading was strictly regulated: state monopolies were established for certain forms of merchandise and duties were exacted on sales, up to thirty per cent of the value of the articles. China, in short, was a wealthy nation.

On the military front, however, Song China was incapable of defending itself. The conquest undertaken by Genghis Khan at the beginning of the thirteenth century was completed in 1279 and China fell under the Mongol yoke.

The **Yuan dynasty (1279–1368)** was founded by a Mongol conqueror. Kublai Khan, at the head of his warriors – who were far less savage and ferocious than the hordes of his father Genghis Khan – subjected the whole territory of China for the first time to foreign domination. Hardly was the invasion of China complete when the Mongols launched out, not always successfully, on expeditions abroad. The empire grew to an immense size.

Kublai Khan, the first Yuan emperor, established peace throughout the land. The caravan routes, not used since the T'ang age because of the risks they entailed, were once more opened. A network of relays, 'more than ten thousand', according to Marco Polo, could accommodate and supply fresh horses to official inspectors or ordinary travellers. Affluent merchants contributed to the development of the great towns and to the growth of the economy. Even Europeans, profiting from the security that the Mongols guaranteed throughout their vast empire, travelled the Silk Road. Marco Polo was the only visitor to the East to narrate his experiences in a book, *The Description of the World*, better known today as *The Travels of Marco Polo.*

Decorative patterns to suit the taste of clients in the Middle East: above, arabesques of peonies; right, flowers often represented on pieces in this style. They may be used together, with or in place of peonies, or even alone.

Completely imaginary, these 'India flowers' are very decorative. Use the arabesques to adorn a very broad horizontal band on the belly of an open vase or a vase with a separate cover

Marco Polo accompanied his father and uncle, both Venetian merchants, on a second journey to China. Leaving in 1271, they did not return until 1295. Marco Polo spent this time in the service of Kublai Khan. Granted high office, he was a privileged and highly perceptive observer. These enormous, well-organised towns, this immense population, the pomp of the palaces and life at court, the efficiency of the administration, were all cause for marvel, even though he was a sophisticated Venetian. The son of merchants, he was very attentive to everything connected with trade and left detailed descriptions of business procedures.

According to tradition, he brought the first pieces of porcelain to Europe, including a white vase belonging to the Treasury of St Mark's, Venice. It is highly probable that other pieces reached Europe via exchanges of gifts and embassies with Egypt and other Islamic countries, but it is difficult to confirm this.

Marco Polo described this porcelain and its uses: 'Let me tell you about their money: they pay in white porcelain (cowries), i.e. the sea-shells that are used to make necklaces for adornment ...; eighty cowries are equivalent to one *saggio* of silver, which is worth two Venetian groats, and eight *saggi* of fine silver may be taken to equal one of fine gold.' (*The Travels of Marco Polo*, Chapter CXIX.)

'Let me tell you further that in this province, in a city called Tinju, they make bowls of porcelain, large and small, of incomparable beauty. They are much appreciated everywhere for they are made nowhere else except in this city, and from here they are exported all over the world. In the city itself they are so plentiful and cheap that for a Venetian groat you might buy three bowls of such beauty that nothing lovelier could be imagined. These dishes are made of a crumbly earth or clay that is collected by the citizens which is dug as though from a mine and stacked in huge mounds and then left untouched for thirty or forty years exposed to wind, rain and sun. By this time the earth is so refined that dishes made of it are of an azure tint with a very brilliant sheen.' (The city in question was present-day Longquan in southern Chekiang, land of celadons. *ibid*, Chapter CLVIII.)

The Yuan emperors were not lovers of art and gave it no special support. They were nevertheless highly interested in profitable international trade. To increase this they encouraged the development of craftsmanship and in particular the expansion of the ceramics industry. Porcelain, highly valued and in great demand, gradually came to occupy a prime place in maritime commerce. Its production was stepped up at Jingdezhen (Ching-tê-Chen), seat of great porcelain workshops since the Song era, which became one of the most important manufacturing centres in China. But the beauty of the objects, as reflected in the perfection of form and glazing, was no longer the prime objective. Sobriety was replaced by ever richer decoration painted in underglaze cobalt blue, executed with great mastery and entirely covering the pieces in conformity with the taste of important clients in the Indies and the Middle East. This readiness

to respond to the customers' tastes stimulated research into new forms and techniques. It was a period of new, varied, coloured and sumptuous production, diametrically opposed to the discrete and refined beauty of the great Song ceramics.

Despite the lack of interest of the Yuan emperors in art, their period was distinguished by considerable cultural activity and especially by the works of the scholar–painters who, having retired to the country so as not to be beholden to the conquerors, painted in intimate surroundings and for pleasure. Those painters who remained in court service worked in the academic style, which at that time exerted great influence on porcelain decoration.

The Yuan period was difficult for the population of China. Apart from those who collaborated with the occupiers, others had to fill subordinate posts or serve as troops for the numerous military expeditions, and their lands were confiscated by the Mongols. People in the countryside suffered extreme poverty and conditions eventually led them to rise in rebellion. These events culminated in the overthrow of the Yuan dynasty.

# Blue-and-White Porcelain

■ Large bowl
Design by R. Van der Broek

During the Song era a new type of decoration for porcelain was introduced, namely a cobalt blue underglaze which underwent a single firing. Under the Yuan dynasty this style was developed and perfected, characterising a significant sector of the Chinese porcelain industry.

The painting of attractive blue-and-white patterns demanded extreme dexterity on the part of the decorator. In its original form, the piece was shaped from a very dry but unfired porcelain paste. On this highly porous and absorbent, blotter-like surface, he drew and painted his motif in water-thinned colour. Each line or brush stroke had to be definitive, with no room for error. When the decoration was finished, the piece was covered with a fine layer of glaze and was finally fired at a very high temperature (about 1400°C), which transformed the paste into porcelain and vitrified the glaze.

The major part of the production was destined for export and the decoration was conceived above all to satisfy a clientele from the Middle East. The composition was dense, arranged in borders, horizontal lines and panels, so as to occupy virtually the entire surface. The varied motifs included sinuous dragons, flying phoenixes, flowers, landscapes, etc.

Native cobalt blue probably contained impurities and had a dull, greyish colour. When the cobalt was imported from the Middle East, the blue became much richer and deeper.

Not only did the blue colour on Chinese pieces vary according to the quality of the cobalt employed, but there were also considerable nuances in tone. This was due to the technique of underglaze painting, very similar to painting in ink and watercolour, which allowed for graduated wash tints. It was also possible, in order to increase the depth of tone, to accumulate colour and to achieve a so-called 'heaped' or 'piled' effect of relief. Such effects are very risky, indeed well-nigh imposssible, when painting on porcelain.

Blue-and-white designs are still in great demand today. They are turned out on a massive scale by the porcelain industry and constitute excellent models for anyone interested in the art of porcelain painting. The dragon, the phoenix and the peony are among the most ancient motifs, and were originally engraved or carved in relief prior to being painted. The subjects represented here are grouped according to theme. To provide a little more colour, we have included several motifs that were created at a later date, but they are compatible with the methods and techniques practised during this period.

▨ Dragon, in black and white, various patterns of clouds to fill in a decorated surface

▨ Right: Chinese warriors and motifs to complete the decoration of the vase shown on page 15

## DRAGONS

According to legend, the dragon was the actual originator of the nation, which explains why it was held in such veneration. It was also the symbol of the emperor.

The dragon was a mythical creature which combined the features of several animals: the head of a camel, the ears of a cow, the horns of a gazelle, the body of a serpent covered with the scales of a carp, and the claws of an eagle.

Usually depicted in a setting of waves, the dragon, as legend relates, emerged from the deep, muddy waters and reared up towards the sky in search of spiritual perfection. Gliding through the clouds, it pursued a magic pearl which conferred universal power. For some this ball represented the sun, which the dragon attempted, unsuccessfully, to swallow. The figure of the creature was often painted on the doors of the houses of judges and important officials and on the porcelain wares designed for these dignitaries.

Close scrutiny of these painted dragons reveals a curious detail that distinguishes the origin of the pieces: on those made by the state factories the dragons have five claws: on the porcelain from private workshops, they sre shown with only three or four claws.

The dragon is a very decorative subject and easy to paint. It suits all kinds of objects (boxes, teapots, pin-trays, etc) and plates and vases of all sizes. It is best to choose typically Chinese or plain, uncomplicated forms.

The dragon is often represented folded back on itself, and this position is suitable for rounded compositions (bottom of a plate, lid or box cover).

Shown standing erect, the dragon can decorate one face of a vase. The opposite side can be painted with a text in Chinese characters or, if preferred, another dragon.

Represented lying lengthways, alone or in pursuit of another dragon, it can be used as decoration for a bowl or cup, perhaps occupying a horizontal band around a vase or potiche (vase with separate cover).

Do the dragon design in several stages, as follows:

1 Position the motif. Draw or transfer the dragon, without the scales and other details which can be added later.
2 Draw the model with a pen and this time add all the details.
3 Apply colour:
   a) Colour and make uniform by tinting the broader surfaces such as the dragon's body.
   b) If, on the model concerned, the scales of the dragon have a white border, these must be coloured individually. Fix the colour by firing.
4 Retouch to deepen the colours in places as required and re-fire.

The dragons can be coloured red, green, or deep yellow on a red background, in polychrome.

Always use two colours: a dark one for the drawing and the dark parts, and a pale one for painting the light parts. To draw a yellow dragon, use black.

The design of a large piece such as a vase, for example, comprises several decorative motifs, including bands, fillets and borders. Some of them frame the principal subject, others serve to finish the piece. They are done in the same way and with the same colours. So all the decorative parts proceed together step by step. The work can be made easier by means of intermediate firings between drawing, colouring and retouching, but these should not be done randomly. It is worth remembering that Chinese decorators, unless painting or gilding on the glaze, have always made do with a single, definitive firing, without any opportunity to wipe out or correct. Multiple firings and simple oversights often result in unexpected and undesirable variations of colour. To avoid this fault, it is always useful to make a note of the colours employed.

The dragon is a simple subject and very suitable for beginners. However, it entails a great deal of pen work and also demands delicacy and precision of line. It is preferable, therefore, to acquire the knack of this technique before attempting this type of design.

The great classic models are there to be copied either for the sake of learning, for reasons of taste or for lack of personal ideas. Whatever the motive, it is an excellent exercise and the result, if the work is properly done, always gives satisfaction. The older examples can also serve as a source of inspiration for the creation of new models and new interpretations; and if the idea is sound and the execution correct, the pleasure is all the greater.

## FRUITS

For a beginner, the plate is the best choice for porcelain painting: it is convenient in size, easy to handle and, because of its resemblance to a flat sheet of paper, not too unfamiliar in shape.

The techniques used in the model represented are basic and extremely simple: transferring, pen drawing and flat colouring.

▦ Dragon plate
Design by A. Mattei

intense and brilliant. Rely on taste and instinct. The suggested motifs can be used, too, for making designs that are not Chinese. Simply change the flowers for everyday garden species and colour appropriately, thereby completely transforming the originals.

These subjects all begin with a pen drawing. The colour of the leaves is almost uniform but that of the petals is graduated. Obtain this effect:

- by tinting with a brush or small pad. The graduation is very regular, and the surfaces have a velvety look.
- when the petals are small, beginning at the spot where the colour is deepest: turn the brush slightly, colour across from left to right, achieving a shaded effect by leaving either the tip or the base of the petal white or with only a dab of paint.

Reinforce the stems and ornamental foliage with the brush.

## The symbolism of flowers

The peony has been the queen of flowers ever since it was so named in a poem of the Tang dynasty. It is a symbol of wealth and nobility, but also of feminine beauty, love and affection. Represented with many leaves, it foretells luck and good fortune.

The lotus, which rises from the mud to bloom in its full beauty, is the symbol of purity and perfection.

## LANDSCAPES

'It is easy to paint a mountain in fine weather, or in rain. It is much more difficult to seize that moment between being and non-being, when fine weather is on the point of giving way to rain, or, vice versa, when rain begins to clear and give way to fine weather. Or again when, bathed in morning mist or dusky smoke, objects are plunged into half-shade, still distinct but still suffused with an invisible halo which unites everything.'

Ch'ien Wen-shih (Song dynasty)

The landscape is one of the great themes of Chinese painting. Between the Tang and Song eras this genre reached its complete development. The landscapists followed the two principal trends that distinguish this form of art: the masters of the North excelled in the realistic treatment of the subject, those of the South interpreted it more poetically and at the same time emphasised the truly human dimension, confronted by the grandiose spectacle of nature. Towards the end of the Song era the tradition of the scholar–painters appeared. Wang Wei (701–61), one of the most celebrated artists and calligraphers of his time, is regarded as the author of this genre and of monochrome painting. 'His paintings were poems and his poems were paintings'; this commentary on the work of Wan Wei helps to explain his impact and the tendency he initiated.

These landscapes are monochrome

and painted in ink, a technique which does full justice to the meditative approach to nature exemplified by so many Chinese painters.

The influence of ink painting was strongly evident in the black-and-sepia landscapes painted on porcelain, although this form of decoration was only created later, when the colour black was introduced at the beginning of the eighteenth century. Experiments had been made with black glaze, but the result was usually leaden and thus short-lived. In cases where it succeeded, analyses revealed that the wash of black glaze was protected by a thin layer of transparent green glaze, a delicate and expensive technique, which consequently was very little used.

During the Yuan epoch the landscapes which appeared as a decorative element on porcelain were painted in underglaze cobalt blue. They were copies of paintings that illustrated both trends, but these reproductions were highly stylised. This treatment makes the genre particularly accessible to beginners.

### Practical advice

Select the position for the landscapes on the piece to be painted. Do the outlines with the pen in dark blue and then colour the subjects. It is very important to catch the spirit, the fleeting atmosphere, of the Chinese landscape. Tint whenever necessary to soften the colours. Fire before retouching the details and darkening the colours.

Landscapes are often used for decorating vases. On a rounded or many-sided vase, the panoramic landscape (suitably enlarged beforehand to the required scale) can go right around the piece. If the vase is square, divide the landscape into two sections and paint each of the two on opposite faces. A perfect way of completing the landscape decoration is to add a vertical inscription in Chinese characters, true to the spirit of the early scholar-painters.

'The ancients were in the habit of representing trees in groups of three, five, nine or ten. They painted them in

their various aspects, each according to its distinctive appearance; they blended the uneven heights of their silhouettes into a living, harmonious whole. I like painting pines, cedars, old acacias and junipers, often in groups of three or five. Like heroes performing a war

In both Chinese and European landscape painting, trees, diminutive in the distance and looming large in the foreground, enliven and often dominate the composition. Contrary to appearances, however, it is not easy to draw a tree convincingly; sometimes an otherwise skilfully executed work may be ruined by a clumsily managed tree. Before attempting a tree motif, examine and analyse the model carefully. Once the essential lines are grasped, the subject can be reproduced faithfully. This preparatory stage is especially important when drawing subjects freehand. It is equally valid for transfer work because when this is done in a rough and ready fashion, or too hurriedly, the result is all too often stiff, awkward and ugly.

dance, they display a wide variety of attitudes and gestures; some lower their heads, others raise them; some double up on themselves, others point straight and boldly upward.'

Shih T'ao (Ming dynasty)

# ISLAMIC ART

# History of the Islamic World

The Middle East, situated at the junction of the European, Asiatic and African continents, is one of the most ancient cradles of humanity. This crossroads has attracted people of diverse origins and natures, and has witnessed a succession of cultures – Sumerian, Chaldean and Egyptian, and has been influenced by many forms of art – Graeco-Roman, Byzantine, Chinese, Hindu and that of the Steppes.

In the seventh century AD a new state appeared in Arabia which developed rapidly and expanded into a vast empire. This civilisation imposed strict religious laws which governed every sphere of life, including society and the arts.

Arabia, nevertheless, did not introduce an autonomous form of art to its conquered lands. It assimilated their cultural heritage, together with their materials and techniques, modifying them in the light of their own spiritual beliefs.

The rich, varied and specifically Islamic style of art that had its origins in the religious and political history of this fertile region was to flourish for approximately one thousand years, showing no signs of decline until around the end of the eighteenth century.

Islamic art had its foundations in the religious and political history of the Middle East. Islam is a monotheistic religion, founded by Mohammed in the seventh century in Arabia. Its preaching, as well as a body of prescriptions designed to control the lives of Muslims (*muslim* means 'believing'), are assembled in the Koran.

Mohammed belonged to the Quraish clan, which had settled around Mecca and which ruled that city. Initially, his teaching aroused the hostility of the clan and he was compelled to flee to Medina, where he succeeded in establishing a state with a social framework rooted in obedience to Koranic law.

He instituted the holy war (*jihad*) which imposed on every Muslim the duty to combat infidels in order to convert them and force them to pay tribute. This led to the expansion of Islam. After the death of the Prophet, large-scale expeditions were carried out beyond Arabia, and an immense empire was established within less than a century.

The Muslim religion spread like wildfire. Part of the success of Islam may be attributed to the discontent of populations exhausted by the excesses of taxation and the spendthrift policies of Byzantium. The policy of military conquest continued unabated, and by 700 the empire extended to India and central Asia to the east, and to the west as far as Spain. The Arab invasion of Europe was finally checked by the forces of Charles Martel at Poitiers in 732, but the Arabs did not abandon Narbonne until 759.

The Koran played a capital role in imposing upon the new territories not only political order but also the Arabic language and Islamic culture. It also became a unifying factor throughout the entire empire.

**The Omayyad dynasty** (661–750). After the death of Mohammed, the sovereigns of the Muslim state bore the title of caliph. The Omayyad and Abbasid caliphs, the first two dynasties, were originally of Quraich stock and related to Mohammed.

Medina was the political centre during three caliphates. The first dynasty, that of the Omayyads, transferred the capital to Damascus, which occupied a central place in the territories newly conquered by Islam.

The Omayyads were great builders. They erected imposing mosques which symbolised Islam. They also made a display of their wealth and power by constructing seats of government in sumptuous palaces and princely residences, known today as 'castles of the desert'.

Architecture depended on local trades and provided the impetus for craftsmanship and the arts in general. Economically and commercially, it was a prosperous period, but nevertheless not a time of untroubled calm.

The empire was shaken by perpetual crises due to the political instability of the Arabs who were organised into rival tribes, to religious divisions (Shiites, Sunnites and other sects) and to the social injustices suffered by non-Muslim Arabs. A revolt overthrew the caliph and all the members of his family were wiped out. Abd-al-Rahman escaped the massacre, fled and founded the independent emirate of Cordoba.

The ceramics of this first period consisted only of utilitarian pottery. The nomadic lifestyle of the tribes from the desert restricted their needs for portable and functional objects. On the other hand, it developed the taste for decorating such pieces, and this is evident from the abundant ornamentation of ceramic ware.

**The Abbasid dynasty** (750–1258), descended from an uncle of Mohammed, came to power with the support of the Shiites of Persia and Mesopotamia. The powerful bureaucracy thus established relied upon a non-Arab Muslim army. This consisted principally of Turkish soldiers, known for their military prowess, recruited from the Turkish tribes which poured in under the pressure of Mongol expansion into Asia.

The new dynasty decided to change the site of the capital. Consequently it built Baghdad and Samara, the short-lived ninth-century capital. The finest artists and craftsmen were called in so that these cities could be more beautiful and sumptuous than their antecedents.

The taste for luxury and the needs of the court stimulated trade, and art objects, silks, precious stones and porcelain flowed in from the Far East. This was the era of Haroun al-Rashid (786–809), monarch and protagonist of the *Thousand and One Nights*, who led a legendary life in his dream palaces crammed with fabulous wealth.

Ceramics occupied a very important place among the professions. One of the reasons was probably a prophetic text to this effect: 'The fire of hell will certainly thunder like the roar of the camel in the belly of whomever eats or drinks from the vases of gold and silver.' Thus in the wealthiest houses table services were of ceramic (earthenware, faience or porcelain) and tinned copper. Everyday receptacles and utensils were made of earthenware and decorated principally with painted slip.

Among the most remarkable objects are the Samanid ceramics, dating from the period of the **Samanid dynasty,** (819–1005), with its capital of Bokhara in Transoxiana. These are decorated with Kufic inscriptions in brown or black slip on a ground of white slip.

In ninth century Mesopotamia, Muslim potters discovered the technique of tin-glazed faience. Around the same time, ceramics with a metallic play of colours made their appearance. These pieces were painted, glazed and fired once, then covered with a varnish containing silver, copper and other metals. They were then fired at low temperature, but in a reducing atmosphere which transformed the varnish into an iridescent film. This type of glittering decoration was already a feature of glass manufacture in Egypt. In Iran the technique was adapted and applied to faience; it was to spread rapidly throughout the Islamic world.

With time, the energy and influence of the Abbasids crumbled. Peasant revolts and uprisings provoked by religious dissidents weakened the central government.

In various parts of this immense empire local dynasties seized power. Some were vassals of the Abbasids, others instituted independent states, such as Transoxiana, Afghanistan and eastern Iran under the Samanids, the emirate of Cordoba, and the caliphates of the Maghreb and Egypt. Even in Baghdad the Abbasid caliph lost temporal power in 1055 and only retained his religious authority.

**The Seljuk dynasties** (1055–1243): Around the end of the tenth century, the Seljuk Turks, originally from Transoxiana, began to emigrate westward. In 1055 the grandson of Seljuk, Togrul, had himself crowned by the caliph of Baghdad. The new dynasty, converted to Islam, assumed the role of protectors and inheritors of Abbasid culture; it would rule the Muslim East from the eleventh to the thirteenth century. A major victory over the Byzantines at Manzikert (1071) enabled the nomadic Turkish tribes to spill out into the whole of Asia Minor. It was this advance of the Turks into the Holy Land that sparked off the great adventure of the Crusades.

The reigns of the first three Great Seljuks ushered in a period of peace and economic prosperity. They built several capitals consecutively (Konya, Isfahan) and covered Anatolia with monuments. They founded and constructed *madrasas* (Islamic universities); they raised mausoleums, observatories and *khans* (fortified caravanserais) along the great caravan routes leading from the East. All large towns had their mosques, hospitals and Turkish baths. The encouragement of intellectual and cultural activity fostered progress in the sciences, the arts and the professions.

Industry and, in particular, ceramics, much in demand as architectural ornament, experienced unprecedented growth.

While known techniques were perfected, new, improved ones were introduced. The most important was the discovery in Iran of white-paste ceramics, which made it possible to decorate pieces without applying slip. This was a white frit which was fired at a high temperature, and the decoration was in two or three colours, greens, blues and black. The pieces were then covered with a transparent alkaline glaze, another innovation, which fixed well both on frit and on pastes of

■ This motif comes from a fragment of a bowl made in Syria or Egypt in the fourteenth century and has lost nothing of its beauty and decorative value. The motif covers the entire piece and all the spaces between the vegetable elements of the background are filled with fine hatching and geometrical shapes. Use this design in monochrome, in polychrome or in one colour (black, red, etc.) and in gold for the lid of a large rectangular or square box, for the bottom of a tray or an ashtray. It can be very impressive as a large frieze on a tall, very simple form

Motifs from Iznik based upon decorative Seljuk flowers

mixed composition. This latter type of ceramic ware could be decorated either with overglaze or underglaze.

Towards the end of the twelfth century a new type of design was developed, known by the name of *haft-rang* ('seven colours' in Persian) or *mina'i*, which derives from *mina*, the Persian for 'glaze'. It was done in two firings. The slipped pieces were painted in pale blue, green or turquoise, covered with a transparent glaze and fired. Then the motifs, drawn in black and coloured red, yellow, brown and blue, were fixed with a second firing at 800°C. This temperature made it possible to use more oxides and thus a richer range of colours. It was the most frequently employed technique for the production of tiles during the Seljuk period.

In the homes of imperial dignitaries, the walls were decorated not only with abstract designs but also with figurative compositions. Subjects, probably inspired by Islamic manuscripts, represented people, dogs, birds and other animals. Humans were shown straddled or seated cross-legged. This manner of sitting, called 'the Turkish fashion', was introduced from Asia and in Islamic art it was the symbol of an easy life. Certain figures bore an aureole as a sign of nobility. The sphinx, harpies and other legendary images harked back to the shamanism of the Turks of Central Asia. Taken in conjunction, these motifs, painted in sparkling, brightly coloured enamels, constituted the most original creation of the Seljuk period. Another new architectural feature was the introduction of mosaic in the form of cut ceramic squares.

**The Mongol and Il-Khan dynasties** (1215–1353): In 1206 Genghis Khan was ruler of all the nomadic Mongol tribes. He carved out a state and, at the head of an immense army, embarked on a campaign of conquest. First he subjugated northern China, then Afghanistan and eastern Iran, pillaging towns and slaughtering entire populations. It was the Seljuks who succeeded in checking the Mongol advance in Syria.

On the death of Genghis Khan (1227), his vast empire was shared out between the Yuans in China and the Il-Khans of Iran. The fall of Baghdad in 1258 put paid to the Abassid caliphate, but at the end of the century the Il-Khans, converts to Islam, were completely integrated. Their very close relations with the Yuan sovereigns brought a strong Middle Eastern influence to the artistic field, just as the impact of Islam made itself felt in China.

Tamerlane and the **Timurid dynasty** (1370–1507): Some time after 1330, a Turkish Muslim adventurer, Timur i Leng (Tamerlane), a native of Kesh near Samarkand, freed Transoxiana from the Mongols and attempted to build an empire. Leaving destruction everywhere in his wake, he reached Ankara where in 1402 he won an important victory over Bayazid I, the Ottoman sultan. His empire, nevertheless, was short-lived. After Tamerlane's death in 1405, it was divided between his descendants.

The Timurid princes began to rebuild the regions Tamerlane had devastated. They were aesthetes and patrons, but politically weak, and gradually they were stripped of power. Herat, capital of Tamerlane's fourth son, Shahruk, became an important centre of art and culture.

These monarchs, ardent book-lovers, founded a library with a separate painting studio, famed for its miniatures.

After the technical progress and decorative variety of the Seljuk period, ceramics went into something of a decline. Nevertheless, enamelled tiles and ceramic panels were still produced abundantly and used for architectural decoration.

From about 1400, empires were set up in the Islamic world which were to last several centuries.

The Ottoman empire was founded by Turkish princes belonging to a small emirate of Anatolia. Constantinople fell in 1453 and, under the name of Istanbul, became the capital of a territory extending to Hungary in Europe, the Caucasus in Asia and Algeria in Africa. The Safavids came from Azerbaidjan and settled in Khorassan, with Isfahan as their capital. The dynasty of the Grand Moguls established its empire, together with Islam, in India. After the Spanish defeat of the Moors at Granada in 1492, Tunisia, Algeria and Morocco were governed by local Ottoman dynasties.

Historical events greatly influenced the development of the arts in these regions. The culture of Islam, transmitted through the concepts, the language and the calligraphy of the Koran, was a unifying force. But later, as the empire gradually disintegrated, regional characteristics took hold, producing diversity within the framework of uniformity.

The civilisation of Islam created a readily identifiable art form. Both in the domain of architecture and of the minor arts, surfaces were generally covered with an abundance of decoration. Arabic writing was often one of its elements, but even when it was not employed, every theme in an extremely rich decorative repertory revealed its cultural attribution.

## ARCHITECTURAL CERAMICS

Islamic civilisation was notable for its large-scale architectural activity. In this vast empire there were many capitals, not all of which have been mentioned in this brief survey. Each dynasty aimed to have its own, and some had several, as in the case of the Ottomans (Iznik, Bursa and Edirne prior to Istanbul). All these capitals had to be furnished with houses, civic buildings, monuments and palaces, and also had to reflect the wealth and power of the caliphs and sultans.

■ Facing tiles, Iznik, c. 1580. The motif consists of four parts. The large almond-shaped cartouches have a red ground which highlights tulips, pinks and roses. The long 'Saz' leaves, as well as the prunus blossom, are on a bright cobalt blue ground and coloured turquoise blue. The tulips on a red ground are white and bright blue, those on a turquoise ground white and red. The leaves are emerald green. While the prunus sprigs are in brown, the other flowers are painted in reserve on coloured grounds

This creative atmosphere stimulated interest in all forms of decoration. Ornamental motifs covered everything from the tiniest household object to an entire building. Outside and interior walls alike were lined with enamelled bricks, mosaics and panels of ceramic tiles.

The incessant demand for architectural decoration kept the ceramics industry fully occupied, and there were periods when virtually all creative activity seemed to be concentrated on this special field.

Less costly than stone or wood and offering unlimited decorative and practical possibilities, lining with ceramic tiles was as widespread in the public sector as it was in the private domain. It was a means of embellishing and personalising a house, and many of those who practised ceramic painting undertook work of this kind. Some restricted themselves to the frieze or to a few painted squares highlighted by a uniform surface; others painted panels, often of considerable dimensions.

■ Indian elephant

## Practical advice

The *frieze* is, as a rule, a repetitive theme. Establish the basic motif on paper measuring the size of the tiles to be decorated. Transfer each part (corresponding to one square) on to tracing paper and number accordingly. Islamic craftsmen who covered entire walls used the pouncing method (see page 172). Before transferring, calculate the number of tiles needed for the whole frieze and do one at a time in a series. If you work with precision, eveything should fit perfectly, but to be on the safe side verify this before firing.

For a *panel*, rule out in squares (each square corresponds to a tile) and number these on tracing paper in proportion to the size of the panel. Draw or transfer the subject, adapted or composed, to the tracing paper. According to the dimensions of the panel and the space available, cut the traced design so as to work consecutively on a small number of spread-out tiles. Before commencing work, number all the tiles on the front with a pencil and on the back with paint.

■ Young man holding an apple in one hand and a glass in the other. In the style of Reza, court painter, Isfahan, Iran, 1615-20
Plaque designed by E. Marshall

Leave aside the painted and dried tiles: pile them up carefully or intersperse them with sheets of paper. Before firing, spread out the whole panel to make any necessary corrections.

## DECORATIVE MOTIFS

One of the major characteristics of Islamic art is the abundance and richness of its ornamentation. Decorative themes of extraordinary variety are based on the repetition and symmetry of the parts, which makes it possible to expand the composition so as to cover the entire surface. This indefinite sequence is based on the arabesque and on geometrical forms.

The arabesque, invented by the Arabs, has its origins in the design repertory of Rome and Byzantium. It adopts the undulating movement of the foliated scroll and has links with the palmette and the soft leaf of the acanthus. The motif of the arabesque reached its classic form in the twelfth century. Under the Seljuks in Iran, these highly stylised elements of vegetation blossomed out into fantastic, gorgeously coloured flowers. In the fourteenth century, under Genghis Khan and his successors, the arabesque, punctuated by lotus and peonies, reflected the growing influence of China. The floral element introduced by the arabesque was to assume capital importance in the art of the Islamic world of the Orient.

Geometry has always been utilised in traditional arts and naturally it inspired and originated much of the ornamentation of the classical world. Islamic art adopted and developed the principle of geometric motifs to the point of culminating in extremely complex and sophisticated compositions.

The division of the circle and the combination of circles made it possible to construct regular polygons and stars. The multiplication and subdivision of these basic forms fostered an infinite number of abstract geometrical motifs.

The techniques of repetition and symmetry provided an opportunity for these juxtaposed and interlaced subjects to expand and cover the entire surface.

Calligraphy, meticulously executed, also served as an ornamental motif and itself became one of the major features of Islamic art.

## ISLAMIC MINIATURES

The importance attached to the Koran, the need to make numerous copies of it and the desire to exalt its sacred character by appropriate ornamentation doubtless contributed to the development of book production. Nevertheless, it was patronage that helped to convert the book into a work of art.

The decoration of the Koran and religious books was restricted to a very elaborate form of calligraphy, to richly illuminated manuscripts and to fine bindings.

Scientific, historical and literary works, which could contain pictures, were abundantly illustrated.

▨ Ashtray
Design by L. Giblain

These illustrations differed greatly according to the style, period and place where they were created. They represented flowers and animals, battle and hunting episodes, genre scenes drawn from daily life, and portraits. Given the quality of composition and excellence of execution, they were paintings in their own right, which were often given the generic name of 'Persian miniatures'.

The art of the miniature began to develop under the Abbasids in Baghdad, but it was the Il-Khan and Timurid princes, great book lovers, who brought it to fruition.

At this time the growing influence of China introduced Chinese motifs into Islamic decoration and the landscape theme into the miniature. Two other schools of painting were equally well known: the school of Mogul India and, more especially, the Turkish school of Istanbul where the Ottoman sultans had gathered together the best calligraphers and painters in the empire.

The technical complexity and virtuosity, the beauty and poetry of these miniatures are a source of endless fascination. Their subjects are very attractive but from the practical decorative point of view they may seem dauntingly difficult. Nevertheless it is possible to find more simple examples suitable for porcelain painting, which, given the necessary precision and patience, are rewarding to copy. These miniatures were painted on paper the size of a book page, and the ornamental porcelain plaque is the ideal piece to show the work to best advantage.

Beautiful pieces can be done, too, in an even simpler fashion. Just select a part of the miniature and interpret it freely by adapting it to the object in hand. The hunting theme was treated repeatedly in Safavid miniatures and it is not difficult to find elephants, hinds and hunters which are very decorative and easy to reproduce.

The young man illustrated on page 43 represents the Islamic artistic conception of idealised beauty: a broad, round face, almond-shaped eyes, a small mouth, full cheeks, a small nose and long hair.

The miniature is framed by two supplementary, flecked borders, similar to the one at the edge of the subject. In the same colour, the second is nevertheless deeper in tone and each is framed in turn by thin frames of gold and coloured fillets.

These details should be noted by those wishing to paint the subject on a larger plaque without altering the dimensions of the central subject.

**Proceed as follows:**

1  Transfer the design on to the plaque. Do the outlines and fine details in pen, the thicker ones with the brush. Work carefully on the face. Do all the lines of the frame in black pen. Fire.
2  Colour the central subject, except for the face, the hands and the background. Tint the turban and robe. Tint the frame. Fire.
3  Protect the subject with resist glaze and tint the background. Do the rough-cast of the frame. Fire.
4  Colour the face and hands by tinting, strengthen the colours if necessary; give it the final appearance. Fire.
5  Carefully do retouching in white. Apply the gold, by beginning with the background decoration, then, successively do the fillet, the rough-cast and finally, the outside fillet before re-firing.

## HISPANO-MORESQUE FAIENCE

In 711 the Muslims conquered almost the whole Iberian peninsula. But this part of the empire quite soon detached itself from Damascus. In 756 an exile from the Omayyad family took refuge in Spain and, under the name of Abd-al-Rahman I, founded the caliphate of Cordoba. At the end of the century a large part of the Maghreb was likewise independent.

At the beginning of the twelfth century rival bands (*taifas*) disputed the caliphate of Cordoba. It disappeared in 1031 and the territory was divided among several small unstable kingdoms.

At the same time, the Berber dynasty of the Almoravids, strict Muslims, reigned over Morocco and the Maghreb as far as Algiers. After the downfall of Muslim Spain, they were called in by the *taifa* kingdoms to check the Christian advance. The Almoravids occupied Spain and in the twelfth century they were replaced by the Almohads, another Berber dynasty.

In the thirteenth century the decline of the Almohad dynasty led to the Christian reconquest, during which all Spanish possessions were recovered. The kingdom of Andalusia, governed by the Nasrid dynasty, was the last outpost of the Moors. In 1492 the capture of Granada ended eight centuries of Muslim domination.

Although the art of ceramics was well developed and flourishing in the Iberian peninsula, it was only after the Moorish occupation that glazed faience appeared.

Faience, as well as the technique of lustres, was discovered some time during the ninth century in Mesopotamia. The conquests of Islam spread these techniques around the Mediterranean basin.

They were introduced to Spain with the Berber invasion and would produce a special ceramic known as Hispano-Moresque faience, virtually the earliest appearance of this form of coloured, glazed earthenware in Europe.

The kingdom of Andalusia was an ideal location for the development of this type of pottery. The construction of the Alhambra in Granada began in 1273 and the palace was gradually covered with extraordinary blue-and-white, polychrome and iridescent faience tiles. The court of the Nasrid kings placed a high value on this sumptuous glazed ware and played an important role in stimulating its production.

**Malaga** Malaga, in Andalusia, became one of the most famous manufacturing centres in Spain. The first lustred faience wares were probably produced there. Since it was also a major port, the celebrated gilded pottery ware of Malaga was exported to the countries of the Mediterranean and even to England.

Particularly well-known examples of this production were the famous Alhambra vases with winged handles. Their

■ This rectangular tile from Iznik from the second half of fifteenth century, is an example of the knotted arabesque, an extremely popular decorative motif. Its author, known as the 'master of the knots', often associated it with other themes, including *tchis*, derived from Chinese clouds
On this tile the design is formed by superimposing a thin arabesque and a thick knotted arabesque. This motif can serve for a cake tray or a square object by taking only the central part. It can also be used wrapped around cylindrical objects (cup, vase, pencil-holder, etc.) or vertically if the object has sides. The design offers a number of ideas for colouring

large size, their original, elegant decoration, and their overall workmanship testify to the considerable talent and mastery of the artists who conceived and designed them.

There were two types of Malaga faience design. In the *obra dorada* (gilded pottery) only the very elaborate motifs and interlacings were gilded. The other type of decoration was based on the contrast of the blue and the glaze on the greyish-white ground of the earthenware.

The decorative style of the Nasrids was very rich. The interior of cups and dishes, often divided into panels, was freely adorned in the Islamic manner with motifs of Persian inspiration. Bands of Kufic characters or separated words, expressing wishes such as 'blessing', 'luck' and 'prosperity', completed the ornamentation.

Production of expensive faience at Malaga kept pace with the decline of the Nasrid dynasty and gradually ceased in the fifteenth century. However, the workshops of Malaga survive to this day, even though they now turn out ordinary utilitarian ware.

**Manises** From the fourteenth century the potters of Malaga settled in other regions of Spain, introducing their special skills and experience to local workshops. At Manises, a suburb of Valencia, the techniques and designs of Malaga were soon being imitated so successfully that it is often difficult to distinguish the products of the two towns. The decline of Malaga was highly advantageous to Manises, for there was no slackening of interest in the gilded faience produced there.

The potters of Manises produced a wide variety of wares: pots for ointments and *albarelli*, jars and tankards, open and covered vases, jugs and bowls for washing hands, fruit-stands, soup plates and large dishes, as well as a varied selection of objects for everyday use – a list that indicates the potential range of pieces suitable for decoration in this style.

Yet the influence of Islamic art was not restricted to the period of the conquest: the splendour of the Ottoman court and the passion for exoticism during the eighteenth century would produce *turqueries*, which might be mistaken for *chinoiseries* were it not that the figures represented wore turbans. In the nineteenth century these motifs were widely copied or adapted in accordance with European tastes.

▦ From 1560 one colour marked the production of Iznik: an extraordinary, unmistakable red. This was accompanied by equally brilliant colours from deep emerald green to bright blue. Use this model in the same manner as the preceding design

# The Ceramics of Iznik

I znik was the name that the founder of the Ottoman dynasty gave to Nicaea when he made it his capital in 1331. It was already a town with a prestigious cultural and artistic past. In 1402 it was sacked by Tamerlane and it held little interest for subsequent travellers from the West who passed through it.

Iznik possessed all the conditions favourable to the ceramics industry: an ancient tradition of pottery and an abundance of all necessary materials (wood, water and clay). The Byzantine technique was replaced by the traditional Ottoman frit pottery and for about two centuries Iznik became a major centre of ceramic production. The prodigious growth of this industry was due to its proximity to Istanbul. The construction of new palaces, religious buildings and residences created a need for tiles, and the wealthy citizens were eager to buy beautiful tableware.

The Ottoman sultans, in fact, sent their orders to Iznik. During the festivities, lasting fifty-two days, which celebrated the circumcision of Prince Mehmed, 541 pieces of Iznik ware were bought to complete the Chinese porcelain service which had proved insufficient for the large number of guests. Again, Murad III ordered from Iznik 1033 pieces for the receptions in honour of his daughter's marriage. In the reign of Suleiman the Magnificent, who was a great builder, the potters of Iznik were obliged to relegate the production of tableware to second place in favour of facing tiles for the building trade. The ceramics of Iznik were among the finest productions of Islamic art and immediately in great demand. The pieces offered by the sultans and vizirs to foreign ambassadors, the wares acquired by collectors, and the objects brought home by travellers soon spread their reputation through Europe. Iznik also had quite an important foreign clientele, consisting mainly of families from Italy (notably from Florence, Venice, Rome and Mantua) and from Dalmatia, who commissioned large armorial services. Even in the 1560 wardrobe inventory of the Medicis, there was mention of the 'ware of Salonich, similar to porcelain', which suggests this was the 'blue-and-white' of the Ottoman production of Iznik.

From the seventeenth century, however, a worsening economic and political situation led to a slowing down of great building enterprises and a diminished demand for facing ceramics. Moreover, the Ottoman court was increasingly attracted by European art and its orders to Iznik dwindled significantly. Without court support, many workshops disappeared or were compelled to work, more cheaply, for a less demanding clientele. Quality began to decline and with it departed the glorious days of Iznik ceramics.

The technique practised at Iznik was that of painted underglaze decoration. The white tiles produced during this period were richly decorated, sometimes even gilded. But the first pieces of pottery produced at Iznik were red. After being coated with white slip the pieces were left in the sun to dry. The painter–artist used pouncing to trace certain motifs with carbon powder and then painted the basic metallic oxide colours with a brush. The pieces were given a layer of transparent and uncoloured alkaline-lead glaze before being fired at 900°–1250°C. This type of ware, somewhat heavy and commonplace, was quite rapidly abandoned. Thanks to the interest in ceramics shown by Mehmet II and his supporters, the Iznik potters managed to produce pieces with a white body that were worthy imitations of Chinese porcelain.

Iznik ceramics owed their success to their lively, deep tones. Yet the palette was not rich and the colours comprising it were only seven: blue, turquoise, green, black, violet, red and, more rarely, grey. The blue was derived from cobalt oxide from Kashan. Copper oxide produced turquoise or green, according to the composition of the colour and the conditions of firing.

Cobalt oxide and copper oxide had the tendency to spread and overflow, so that to contain them within the desired limits, Ottoman potters used outlines. Until about 1530 these outlines were very dark blue, done in cobalt of such concentration that it was almost in relief and would not fuse. In the 1540s the colours were done in grey-green and from 1550 in black.

Manganese violet was used for some twenty years and then replaced by red.

Underglaze red was one of the hardest colours to obtain. Already used in Islamic ceramics, it appeared dull and brownish in comparison with the glittering red obtained in the seventeenth century at Iznik. The remarkable red of Ottoman potters was derived from a calcareous-ferruginous clay known as 'Armenian bole', an important deposit of which was found in Anatolia, near Kutahya, another important ceramics centre. This clay was well known for its astringent and curative properties: it was used for relieving wounds, particularly those caused by circumcision. Employed thickly on ceramics, this slip of red clay was exceptional in appearance and relief.

Bole, sometimes called *terra miracolosa*, was also known in Italy. At the same period, at Castel Durante, Italian potters used the red of Armenian bole, from a deposit discovered in Tuscany, to decorate majolica.

Several styles marked the products of Iznik. Some designs were borrowed from China, others were common to the Islamic world, but all evolved under local influences. One typically Ottoman style was developed and widely interpreted. This diversity of design and high quality placed Iznik production at the peak of Islamic ceramic art.

### THE OTTOMAN BLUE-AND-WHITE STYLE

Chinese porcelain was greatly appreciated at the Ottoman court. The sultans commissioned it not only as tableware but also for the pure pleasure of collecting it. In fact, during the fifteenth century, the sultans initiated a collection that grew considerably after 1514 when Selim I sacked Tabriz and exacted a vast booty. The imperial palace, Topkapi Sarayi (nowadays transformed into a museum) also housed many masterpieces of Chinese ceramic art.

Topkapi Sarayi also housed workshops where the finest craftsmen in the empire worked. They were furnished with the raw materials they needed, and the quality of their work was closely supervised. The pieces commissioned by the sultan were made here, but it also functioned as a school where craftsmen learned the traditional trades of their choice.

Of all the workshops, the *nakkashane*, devoted to the production of books, was the most important. Miniature painters and book craftsmen created motifs and designs which were then adopted by the other branches of trade. Thus it was in the *nakkashane* that the style which set its mark on the period was born.

A motif that is often found in Ottoman ceramics shows bunches of tulips, daisies, hyacinths and other spring flowers arranged in a vase. It was probably inspired by Chinese models, but is distinguished by the perfect symmetry of the blooms. Often a feature of the blue-and-turquoise group of ceramics, it was also interpreted in polychrome

The Chinese style 'in the Ottoman manner' was called *hatayi* and derived from Kathai (Cathay) in China.

The decoration of the piece on this page was inspired by a lamp of a mosque commissioned by Suleiman for the Dome of the Rock in Jerusalem. The original is in cobalt blue and turquoise highlighted in black and decorated with *tchis* (Chinese clouds) and Koranic inscriptions.

In the adaptation of the model the inscriptions have been omitted and in certain places black is replaced by gold.

**Proceed as follows:**

1 Draw on paper the precise form and size of the dark blue motifs. Transfer on to the piece. Apply resist around the motifs and tint in dark blue. Remove the resist. Fire.
2 Draw with a pen in dark blue the *tchis* on the neck and belly. Colour in turquoise. Fire.
3 Tint in turquoise the bands of the base, belly and neck. Heighten the central motifs if necessary. Fire.
4 Do the motifs in gold. Fire the gold.

The *tchi* has been adopted, transformed and assimilated. It harmonises perfectly with the progress of the arabesque and sometimes, because of its particular shape, is described as 'agraphic'. *Tchis* may be the only decorative element or they may be associated with other motifs.

### THE STYLE OF ABRAHAM OF KUTAHYA

Between 1470 and 1520 a new and specific style appeared and quickly made its mark. It was attributed to Abraham of Kutahya, also known as Baba Nakkash (Venerable Old Master Decorator). He was an Armenian artist of the early sixteenth century, a painter of illuminated manuscripts at the court of Mehmed the Conqueror, and his work was to become the source of this style.

The new style associated the classic, formal structure of Islamic motifs, the arabesque (or *rumi*), with the flowery volute of Chinese porcelains (or *hatayi*). This is why these designs are also called *rumi-hatayï*.

The decorative elements formed complicated compositions which wholly covered the surface of the object, and sometimes they were completed by Kufic inscriptions. The motifs often stood out on an extremely plain blue ground: the cobalt was so thick that it appeared almost black. Objects of this style, but with an inferior paste and design, were described as having been produced in Miletus, having been found on the islands of the Aegean and at Miletus. They were in fact manufactured at Iznik on a bigger scale and for a much larger clientele.

Although at the start the potters of Iznik were requested to copy or imitate Chinese porcelain, the designs created by the masters of the *nakkashane* were soon adopted and influenced the production of ceramics.

A wide range of decorative Chinese motifs was nonetheless employed. Designs incorporating the lotus, the chrysanthemum, the peony and the camellia were adopted and certain themes, such as that of 'waves and rocks' on the wings of plates, became great favourites. The positioning of the design on the dishes and above all on tall pieces where it was arranged in contrasting motifs, remained visibly Chinese-inspired during the blue-and-white period.

The style of Abraham of Kutahya developed and at the beginning of the sixteenth century the motifs were more light and airy: the blue employed was less dark and much of the space was left white.

At the same time the 'knot' and 'cloud' motifs appeared, closely linked with and incorporated into the arabesque style. Objects forming part of this group and long attributed to the pottery workshops along the Golden Horn bear the name of 'Golden Horn' ceramics. Actually they, too, were made at Iznik during the 1530s but they are distinguished from the rest of the production by their decoration. The basic motif is a very simple small flower at the end of a stem with two tiny leaves, which is repeated in the form of a tight concentric spiral. These spirals are attached to one another by medallions and can therefore cover any space. The overall design formed by these motifs is reminiscent of the *tughra*, the imperial monogram of Suleiman the Magnificent, and as a result it is also called the Tughras style.

■ The illustration shows *tchis* which constitute the only decoration of a hollow blue Ottoman dish of 45.5 cm. Their arrangement is as follows:
– within the space marked off by two bands, the decoration comprises the motifs shown in black and white. Divide this circle into six and repeat three times, alternating the large and small motif. The arrangement is in a radiating pattern and the motifs touch the band;
– the border is undecorated in spite of its height;
– on the wing, in a space marked off on either side by a double band (as on the bowl), the elongated *tchi* is repeated five times at equal distances. The outermost bands are slightly less than one centimetre from the edge, which remains white.

This model is not difficult to do and has a lovely effect.

On the dish shown in the plate on page 55, the *tchis*, surrounded by flowers, form a much bolder, richer design

■ Two coffee cups inspired by the Golden Horn style

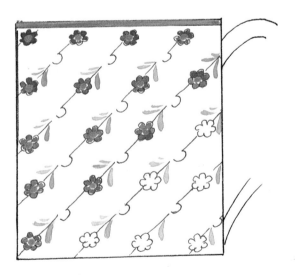

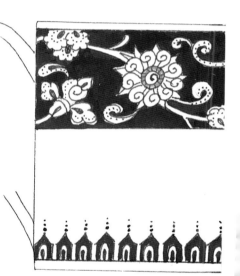

▓ These designs combine the original style of Abraham of Kutahya and simplified adaptations derived from motifs of this style

## THE 'SAZ' STYLE

The 'Saz' style originated in the illustrations of an epic Sassanid work of the fifteenth century. It was introduced into Ottoman art by Shahkoulou, head of the *nakkashane*, who took certain parts of it to create the motifs of this style. One is the Saz leaf which resembles a curved feather or a leaf with toothed margins. Often ornamented with small flowers or white buds, it is supple and vigorous. The other element, rounded and static, is the flower. These huge composite flowers and these blooming rosettes, accompanied by a few buds, bend at the tip of thin, flexible stems, and are distributed over the surface of the piece. This movement and the long curving saz leaves produce lively and dynamic compositions.

The dish shown on page 48 is the copy of a hollow dish forming part of the collection of the British Museum in London. The original is 38.5 cm in diameter and shows a motif typical of the Saz style. These were the stages in its decoration:

1  Taken from a photograph, the subject was enlarged to the required scale by photocopying, and then transferred.
2  The outlines and all the details were applied with a black pen.
3  Colouring was done tone by tone.
4  After firing, some colours were strengthened.

■ Design based on the 'Saz' motif of the dish shown on page 48

The colours used were light blue and dark blue, the two shades being deep and well saturated, and sage green.

The composition is dominated by a tree with a blue trunk surmounted by a large vegetable mass (either an artichoke or a pinecone) covered with scales. This type of design is, in fact, sometimes called 'artichoke' and may contain several of these elements. In contrast to the stiffness of the tree, a swirl of stylised flowers, buds and Saz leaves seems to be breaching the bounds imposed by the border, and some of the flowers are cut in half.

The peacock, an animal motif, is exceptional in the Iznik ceramics of this period.

New flowers now entered the decorative repertory: the rose, open and in bud, the tulip, crocuses and other small spring flowers. The large composite flowers were replaced by other masses of scaly vegetables such as

■ Right: Peacock dish. Hollow dish from Iznik in the 'Saz' style, dated c. 1540: h. 37.5 cm, d. 37.5 cm.
A thin black band in accolades, almost touching the edge, surrounds the motif

derived from manganese), as well as green (ranging from sage to olive), chestnut and grey. Outlines of the motifs, originally green to black, became black during the second half of the century.

### THE 'FOUR FLOWERS' STYLE

The successor to Shahkoulou as director of the imperial *nakkashane* was Kara Memi, who introduced the 'four flowers' style sometimes given his name. In contrast to the Saz style, which focused on the imaginary, the four flowers style was inspired by the real world. The tulip, the rose, the hyacinth and the pink are perfectly recognisable and grow naturally as in gardens. Sometimes the stem is broken and one of the flowers may plunge downward under its own weight, giving a natural, live appearance even when the motif is repetitive. These flower compositions are so characteristic that they readily identify this exclusive Ottoman style, perhaps the most decorative of all and certainly the most highly valued. It introduced a new range of colours that included red and emerald green.

The immediate success of the Kara Memi style was probably due also to the symbolic significance of some of these flowers.

The tulip, according to a contemporary interpretation, occupied pride of place because its name, *lalé*, was the anagram of Allah. But study of the etymology of the tulip and the rose suggests other meanings.

pomegranates,
artichokes or pinecones.
Certain colours employed were rare
and subtle, such as grey, mauve and greens ranging from lime to olive. Blues were deep and highly contrasted. All the drawing was in black.
From 1540 the palette became richer, with the introduction of pale pink, lilac and aubergine (shades

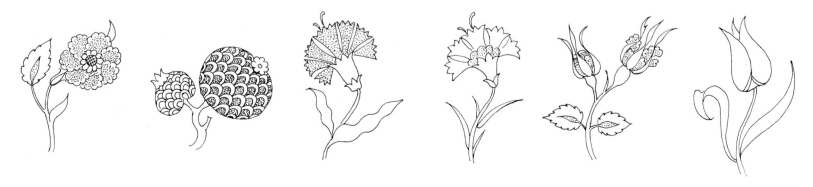

Until the sixteenth century, the Ottoman Turkish term for the tulip was *dülbend lalési*, or 'lalé turban', probably because of the flower's resemblance to a hairstyle. The word *dülbend* became the etymological source of 'tulip' in

different European languages. In Persian and Ottoman Turkish, *lalé* was used at this period as a generic term to signify a wild flower, as against *gül*, which corresponded to a cultivated flower. Then *lalé* began to serve only for wild flowers that were red in colour and it found a place in mystical literature as 'flower of blood' and 'flower of suffering', symbol of the soul and the search for God. It was the emblem of initiation. The cultivated flower, *gül*, symbolised the soul in a state of *baraka*, or grace. A new development made *gül* the specific name of the rose, and *lalé* that of the red tulip and of tulips in general, while retaining their symbolic significance.

Was it the success of the style that contributed to the success of the flower, or vice versa? The fact is that tulip bulbs were sent to botanists, that plates reproducing them were made in many countries, and that this flower, so dear to the Turks, provoked a veritable craze of tulipomania in Europe.

Decoration with human figures appeared around the middle of the seventeenth century. The subject of the illustration on page 60 is derived from a Mogul miniature of the same period portraying a young man reading in a garden, but the treatment is naive and the garden symbolised by a few flowering stems.

This dish was part of the collection of Ottoman faiences set up by Auguste Salzmann, French consul to Rhodes from 1865 to 1878, which was exhibited at Ecouen. The collection, which contained more than 500 pieces, contributed largely to the incorrect description of such wares as Rhodian, whereas they were really products of inferior quality exported at this time by Iznik. The motif of the ship, singly or in a flotilla, appeared around 1530,

sailing boat designs were also found on the Ottoman ceramics that were for a long time incorrectly called 'Rhodian faiences'.

The dominant figure of the Ottoman empire during the sixteenth century was the monarch widely known in Europe as Suleiman the Magnificent. Suleiman came to the throne in 1520, inheriting a vast empire that had gradually been built up since the thirteenth century. In the tradition of the Osmanli warriors, the *ghazis* of the Ottoman state, he personally led his armies in twelve campaigns. He brought the Ottoman empire to its maximum territorial extent and adopted a very threatening attitude towards the Western powers.

Political supremacy was accompanied by an upsurge of artistic and intellectual creativity throughout his domains. Suleiman was not only a man of war – he had great aesthetic sensibility and a taste for luxury. Fascinated by precious stones, he had learned the goldsmiths' craft in the imperial workshops and was a close follower of all their activities. He was particularly interested in book production, for he took pleasure in fine manuscripts and was himself a gifted poet. Under the pseudonym of Muhibbi, 'the lover', he wrote in Persian and Turkish. Suleiman the Magnificent succeeded in harnessing the multiple talents that created and perpetuated a number of very personal and distinctive styles. The period of his rule was in truth the golden age of Ottoman culture.

The wear and tear of family illnesses and problems eventually threw a shadow over the final years of Suleiman's long reign. His last military ventures were failures and he died during the final campaign in 1566. This sad ending to the reign signalled the subsequent gradual decline in Ottoman power and influence.

but for some time remained rarely used. It is a very attractive subject which eventually, when colours were introduced, became part of the regular production. It became popular especially when the Iznik workshops veered towards facile, rapid and economic designs. It was used for plates, pots and tankards.

In some models the central feature of the composition is that imposing ship, the galleon, which covers almost the whole dish. In others the surface is adorned with a flotilla of little boats with lateen sails. They are white on a light green ground, or striped on a white ground. These small boats are arranged in several lines and all facing in the same direction, with little waves or stylised rocks. The

# CHINA: POLYCHROME

# *Historical Background*

■ Preceding double page: the cock, a good omen, shown amid blooming peonies which signify luck, was a very common motif under the Qing dynasty. Done in bright, luminous enamels, it might serve as a central decoration for a plate, for a vase or around the edge of a so-called court bowl. This design was sometimes accompanied by verses which may have been written by the Emperor Qianlong

■ Tea box in the *famille rose* style, decorated with birds and flowering branches. The motif was taken from a piece produced by the imperial workshop in enamel on copper. It was done in three stages:
1 Drawing with the pen and colouring of motifs. Firing
2 Tinting the sides and the stopper, retouching and firing
3 Finishing in gold. Note the delicacy of the drawing and the exquisite workmanship
Design by A. Cassagne

**M**ing dynasty (1368–1644). After a rebellion which overthrew the Mongol Yuan dynasty, its leader, Hong-wou, became the founder of the Chinese Ming dynasty.

The new emperor established his capital in Peking where all administration was centralised. During his reign and that of his son, China experienced a period of political and economic power, allied with territorial expansion and cultural growth.

Important works were undertaken, such as the construction of irrigation canals, public storehouses and the restoration of the Great Wall. Moreover, contacts were resumed and diplomatic relations renewed as far as Turkey, thanks also to the reopening of the Silk Road.

After the death of Tamerlane, tranquillity returned to the Middle East, caravan traffic was re-established and safe communications were guaranteed with inland China.

The Ming emperors aimed to revive trade and between 1405 and 1435 they organised large-scale seagoing expeditions. Tcheng Ho was the first Chinese navigator and explorer successsfully to cross the Indian Ocean. He made seven voyages and established political and commercial relations with India, Persia, Arabia and certain countries on the east coast of Africa. It was a proud exploit for the Chinese who, in spite of their important discoveries in the field of navigation, were not sailors and had left it to Korea and Japan to control maritime traffic. Their junks were not solidly built, and even though those constructed in the Ming period were immense, they remained rickety and not sufficiently reliable to tackle the open sea. The fleet of Tcheng Ho, comprising a dozen of these junks, was impressive and effective. It contributed to the rapid development of trade and especially the export of porcelain, which was much easier

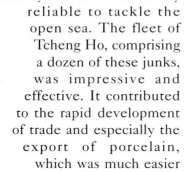

by sea. Thus the renown of China once more crossed sea and land; its prestige and influence are accurately reflected by the name *ming*, which means 'brilliant'. However, around 1450, the situation began to deteriorate. Corruption in the emperor's entourage provoked discontent among the nobility, who plotted and set up secret societies. The condition of the peasants, already harsh, grew worse. In 1512 and 1518 revolts erupted which would destabilise the regime.

Taking advantage of this waning power, the Manchus threw off Chinese sovereignty. Later, the intervention of China on the side of Korea, which had invaded Japan in 1592, brought about systematic reprisals from Japanese pirates along the Chinese coasts. From this time everything conspired against the Ming emperors: a widespread famine in 1640 was followed by revolts of entire provinces. In 1644 the Manchus entered Peking and seized power. The Ming fled to the south of the country but the last emperor was handed over to the Manchus and was executed in 1661.

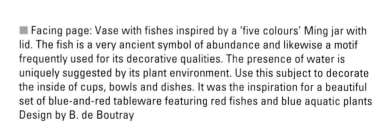

▨ Facing page: Vase with fishes inspired by a 'five colours' Ming jar with lid. The fish is a very ancient symbol of abundance and likewise a motif frequently used for its decorative qualities. The presence of water is uniquely suggested by its plant environment. Use this subject to decorate the inside of cups, bowls and dishes. It was the inspiration for a beautiful set of blue-and-red tableware featuring red fishes and blue aquatic plants Design by B. de Boutray

Despite difficult periods, the reign of the Ming emperors was an era of national revival and brilliant achievement. For the West, the very name of Ming was to become synonymous with porcelain. Yet the first emperor of the dynasty, Hong-wou, was uninterested in the industry and porcelain production stagnated and flagged.

It was only a brief setback, for very soon the town of Jingdezhen, a centre of porcelain production that was already known for its many kilns, was again fully active. It was also a focal point of commerce and remains the principal producer of ceramics in modern China.

Under these auspicious conditions, porcelain made a veritable leap forward. This would be the golden age of blue-and-white and, furthermore, extraordinary discoveries would be made in the field of design. Research and experiment were encouraged by the special interest that certain emperors showed in the art of porcelain. Production of Ming ceramics, extremely rich and varied in style, spanned three centuries.

This was also the period when Westerners flocked to Asia. At the beginning of the sixteenth century Vasco de Gama discovered the route to the Indies and thereafter Europeans assumed control of the maritime trade. Initially the Portuguese and the Dutch, then other Europeans, arrived, set up factories and engaged in busy commerce with China. The product that most interested them was porcelain, and its manufacture grew considerably.

The Portuguese built Macao, which rapidly became an important commercial centre and supply post on the route to Japan. The Jesuits installed a bishopric there in 1557, from which missions departed for China. They were the only Europeans to reach the Chinese court, for official contacts always had been, and still remained, difficult. Finally, in 1601, the emperor invited to Peking Matteo Ricci, a Jesuit well versed in science who had also learned to speak Chinese. The emperor was delighted by the map of the world that Ricci gave him and showed keen interest in European inventions and especially discoveries in the field of astronomy. After Ricci's death, his replacement summoned Terrentius, an associate of Galileo and Kepler, and Schall to instruct the Chinese in that subject. Schall

even became technical adviser to the Ming emperors and his reputation was so great that the Manchus, when they entered Peking in 1644, retained his services.

**Qing dynasty** (1644–1912). The Manchus found their way into China without the use of force. They were called in by Wu Sankouei, a Chinese general, to help pacify a rebellious land. It was a fatal mistake, for the Manchus took advantage of it to remain and set up in power the Manchu Qing (Ts'ing) dynasty.

Conditions in the country were very difficult, and the problems were compounded by the struggles of the pro-Ming legitimists which continued until 1680. These resulted in the destruction of a large part of Jingdezhen. The very limited production during this period of disorder, known by the name of 'transitional porcelain', was destined for export.

Despite these problems, the Manchus managed quite soon to redress the situation. Internal troubles were stifled, corruption disappeared and the lot of the peasants improved. Trade with the outside world was resumed even more actively. China experienced an era of peace and great prosperity that was to last for a couple of centuries.

Moreover, the emperors and their Manchu entourage rapidly adopted Chinese styles and customs. The new dynasty seemed intent upon rivalling the Ming court in refinement and culture. In its turn, too, it patronised the arts.

In the reign of Kangxi (1662–1722) the court became a meeting place for scholars. The emperor was a cultivated man who was tolerant of foreign religions. This was hardly surprising, for the young Kangxi had grown up in an environment of Chinese culture and also had as a teacher Bouvet, known for his universal erudition. The Jesuits were held in increasing esteem for their knowledge and skills which extended to the domain of art. The Jesuit father Giuseppe Castiglione spent most of his life in Peking, directing an imperial workshop of painting, and painted not only for Kangxi but also for his successors, the emperors Yongzheng and Qianlong. The French Jesuits were held in especially high regard. In 1688 France sent a team of scientific missionaries, some of whom were notable as well for their knowledge of Chinese and even of Manchu, and were thus quite at ease in court circles. Ten of them were kept on as advisers. Dominique Parennin, who became a friend of Kangxi, drew up the

celebrated 'Jesuit map' of China, Manchuria and Mongolia, published in Paris in 1735. The emperor even dispatched some of the Jesuits on diplomatic missions; Gerbillon and Pereyra played an important role at Nertchinsk in Siberia and prevented Russia going to war with China.

Francois-Xavier d'Entrecolles, superior general of the French Jesuits from 1707 to 1719, conducted a busy correspondence which contained a detailed description of China. Porcelain was one of the subjects he touched upon. He was very impressed by Jingdezhen, a veritable hive of activity, and also by its working methods and techniques.

Jingdezhen had been burned and partially destroyed during the uprisings. Kangxi even wished to transfer the imperial factory to Peking. He had to abandon this plan because of the long-standing reputation of Jingdezhen as a manufacturing centre of fine porcelain, based largely on the fact that so many of the conditions essential to its success were concentrated in the region. The emperor had the town rebuilt and also appointed an able director who gave a great impetus to production. An extract from a letter written by d'Entrecolles in 1712 provides a striking image of the place:

'After that I cannot avoid giving you, Reverend Father, a description of King-te-Tching. There are large businesses accommodated over a wide area where an enormous number of workmen are employed; it is commonly said that there are more than a million souls, that they consume each day more than ten thousand loads of rice and more than a thousand pigs. For the rest, King-te-Tching extends for a whole league along the banks of a beautiful river... In ancient times, says the history of Feou-leam, there were more than 300 porcelain kilns in King-te-Tching; today there are about 3000. It is not surprising that one often sees fires... King-te-Tching is situated on a plain surrounded by high mountains... The eddies of flames and smoke that belch out in different places give you a good idea of the size and appearance of King-te-Tching; when night falls you would imagine it to be a huge town entirely ablaze, or perhaps an enormous furnace with innumerable vents...'

Kangxi was captivated by all forms of art. Inside the palace he even set up workshops for lacquer, glass, silk painting and enamelling on copper. A Frenchman, Jean-Baptiste Gravereau, introduced the techniques of the French enamellers of Limousin to the imperial studios of Peking.

The emperor was particularly interested in porcelain and his patronage quickly bore fruit. The porcelain of his time was remarkable for its high-quality material, the thematic variety of its decoration and the delicacy of its painting and finishing.

The most outstanding example of porcelain design during this period was the celebrated *famille verte*, notable

▨ Facing page: Vase
Design by M. Braneyre

# Porcelain of the Qing Dynasty

■ The attractiveness of the lotus has never faded over the centuries. These plates are part of a service decorated exclusively with the lotus, adapted or inspired by Chinese silk paintings. The work is done in several stages. After the lotuses have been drawn in grey and the leaf veins in black, the colouring and retouching are done by tinting. Note the extremely painstaking and precise workmanship
Design by H. Petauton

When the Manchus seized power, China's economy was in a bad state. The output of a disorganised porcelain industry was very low and export orders were difficult to fulfil. Thanks to intelligent direction, however, production picked up and quality was immeasurably improved. After the transition period, in the reign of Kangxi, the Wucai and Doucai decorations were eclipsed, first by the *famille verte*, later by the *famille rose*.

### FALANGCAI OR *FAMILLE VERTE* DECORATION
Falangcai decoration originated in the polychrome porcelain of the Ming dynasty, developing and reaching culmination during the reign of the emperor Kangxi.
The name *famille verte* was introduced later by Albert Jacquemart in his history of porcelain, published in 1873.

The immaculate lotus, depicted either in calm or rough water, is the symbol of purity. For this reason it is the sacred flower in India and China and is often depicted as the throne of Buddha.
Lotus design of the Qing dynasty (Kangxi period). The drawing is done in black and red: the background is deep red. However, this motif can be used, wholly or partially, on white, celadon or slightly tinted grounds

The title was determined by the dominant colour of this type of decoration, namely the varied green enamels that were used.

Even so, this name led to confusion. Enamels of this type were also used in the manufacture of pieces with backgrounds wholly coloured in green, yellow or black, unconnected with the true *famille verte*.

The enamels of the *famille verte* were transparent and luminous, their tones fresh and brilliant. They were applied in a fairly thick layer and consequently formed a slight relief perceptible to the touch.

The greens, with a copper oxide base, ranged from very pale to dark, deep emerald.

Antimony yellow was purer and more varied than that employed in previous times.

Aubergine came from manganese oxide. The tone varied, according to the thickness of the enamel, from violet to brown-black.

Iron red, very bright and orangey, was a matt colour and thus not used thickly. It also served for outlines.

The disappearance of turquoise enamel and underglaze blue was the essential difference between Wucai and Doucai decorations.

Underglaze cobalt blue was effectively excluded from the *famille verte* and was replaced by a blue enamel. Difficult to obtain, this was often muddy and violet coloured.

By contrast, black enamel was often present, and gold, used for heightening certain motifs, made its appearance.

Decorative motifs were widely varied. Some, very light and spare, represented what one might describe as the most authentic Chinese taste: a flowering sprig, one or two birds on a branch.

These subjects were more supple, graceful and natural than those of preceding productions. They often reflected the innate compositional sense of the Chinese. Frequently based on extreme asymmetry, the composition was always balanced and harmonious.

Other patterns had the human figure as their subject. The simpler compositions showed several people in a roughly evoked landscape.

From the sixteenth century on, an anecdotal style developed with extremely complex and lively movement, which showed battle and hunting scenes, or depicted religious and historical events.

These designs were organised according to two different conceptions. One, based on simplicity, presented 'solid' subjects on a white ground and occupied the whole surface of the piece.

The other set the subjects inside panels or reserved areas which might take a geometrical, regular form, or which sometimes adopted themes of fruits, leaves, a fan or a *makemono* (elongated roll). These panels and reserves stood out from coloured backgrounds which were sometimes decorated with stylised motifs inspired by brocades and damasks.

The design, quite simple in the early years, became increasingly complex. This overloading is attributed to the inevitable decadence which set in when the search for perfection was pushed to the extreme and it prided itself on its difficulty and virtuosity. It was also much encouraged by dealers in porcelain because it corresponded more to the taste of clients in the Middle East and Europe.

Manufacture was often modelled on a very painstaking and decorative academic style, which can be reproduced, as usual, by pen.

When inspired by the works of the scholar-painters, it was more graphic and spontaneous. The brown-black outlines, applied with or without pressure, and strong cross-hatching, emphasise details, textures and shadows. To be faithful to the spirit and energy that marks this style, it is necessary to employ brushes. The technique is initially as hard to learn as that of the pen, but learning to use brushes with all their potentialities, is essential.

The *famille jaune* is a category of porcelain with a yellow ground. Such wares appeared during the reign of Kangxi.

The *famille noire* derives from the invention at the same period of a brilliant black glaze. The motifs occupy reserves and this contrast gives the colours a marvellously vivid effect.

Strangely, only the pieces painted in iron red and heightened with gold are considered to form part of the *famille verte*.

The prunus with its white, pink and yellow flowers has long been one of the favourite subjects of Chinese painters. It was also the messenger of spring and the symbol of chastity. Down the centuries, cherry, plum and almond blossom has been a decorative motif on porcelain. On the blue plate, branches and flowers are very stylised, forming a lovely covering decoration. This design is very suitable for large pieces. The other plate suggests a very attractive treatment of the prunus theme: the flowers and branches are large in comparison with the object's size, but it is this very fact that makes the model so original and beautiful. The ground is a deep, rich pink

copper, then began to feature in *famille verte* decoration. Despite the great advance in the art of ceramics, purple-pink was totally unknown in China and its use in porcelain was not mastered until 1730. It was to become the characteristic feature of a new style, which succeeded the *famille verte*.

The *famille rose* style was called by the Chinese *fencai*, meaning 'foreign colours' or 'soft colours'. Pink became the dominant colour and was associated with a new palette, inspired by the colour range employed in the imperial workshop of enamels on copper at Peking. The tones, infinitely varied, were opaque. This richness of nuance was due to the matt white arsenic base, also just introduced. It was employed on its own or mixed with enamels so as to obtain an unlimited number of tints.

Typical colours of this category were the pinks, from the palest to ruby-purple, accompanied by lavender blue, mauve, pale green, spring yellow, light red, black and sometimes white.

The decoration, reflecting Chinese taste, was full of grace and poetry. The motifs, taken from nature, brought out the beauty of flowers, of birds hopping about in the branches, of insects and butterflies. The free and natural composition and the extremely refined workmanship were accentuated by the whiteness of the porcelain. There were no borders, nothing to burden or detract from the simplicity and delicacy of these subjects.

Representation of humans was restricted to intimate scenes: pretty young women strolling or resting, playing the zither or the flute, surrounded by children, everything carefully and minutely painted.

The porcelain, too, was of a quality never previously attained. The paste was white, pure, without fault; the glaze perfect. One type of porcelain was so fine and translucent that it was known as 'eggshell'. From this period, too, came the 'ruby back', featuring plates with their reverse side covered with a deep pink and very soft enamel.

## FENCAI OR *FAMILLE ROSE* DECORATION

In the seventeenth century, Andreas Cassius from Leyden in Holland, obtained a new colour, purple, from gold chloride. It was soon adopted in Europe for the painting of ceramics and the enamelling of metal.

Thanks to the Jesuit missionaries, a pink enamel, perfected by German enamellists, was introduced into China around 1720. It was initially used for enamelling on

Prunus branch and bird; brush drawing. This type of composition is described as asymmetrical. Actually this conforms to the notion of Vacuity, a Taoïst philosophical concept adopted by Confucianism and Ch'an (Zen) Buddhism, which is applied to certain practical fields. Without analysing this thought in detail, Vacuity may be said to bring lightness to the composition. Designs of this genre were often employed on 'solid' porcelain, i.e. covering the surface of the piece (plate, vase, etc.) while leaving a considerable white space, the empty area emphasising the motif

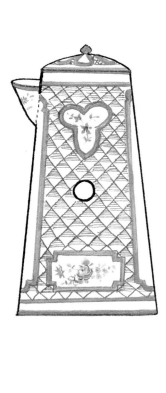

the Equator and, in 1498, Vasco de Gama rounded the Cape of Good Hope and reached India. The route to China now lay open.

## PORTUGAL

Lisbon eventually replaced Venice as premier maritime power. Portuguese navigators, familiar with the sea routes, could now control regular traffic. An important commercial network was built up and factories were established at Calicut and Goa in India. In 1513, for the first time, a European ship made landfall in China. Jorge Alvares opened an embassy in Canton, but relations were difficult and culminated in a diplomatic setback. He even managed to reach Peking but official contacts remained for some time at low level. The Portuguese found their way out of this impasse by offering their aid in the struggle against the pirates who were at this time raiding the south China coasts. In 1557 the emperor rewarded them for this service by giving them the small island of Macao.

The great factories in India and China enabled Portugal to expand its trade, and porcelain was one of the first articles to be exported. The Portuguese passed precise orders to Chinese manufacturers. Armorial services were particularly in demand and supplied even to overseas clients. That of the emperor Charles V, king of Spain, was the first to be made in China.

From 1557 Portugal was governed by weak kings and went through a difficult period. Morocco tried to repel the Portuguese who were ejected from one part of its coast, and the war ended with the defeat of El Ksar-el-Kebir, heavy with consequence for Portugal.

Spain, jealously observing the commercial successes of Portugal, profited from this weakness by invading the country and taking control of trade with the East Indies. Portugal thus found herself annexed to Spain for sixty years.

Lisbon had become the centre of international commerce. Dutch merchants came there to buy Chinese porcelain and resold it in northern Europe. After the annexation, Philip II refused them access to the Lusitanian ports.

Dutch navigators therefore looked for independent routes to obtain direct supplies from China. A fierce struggle, of which the vestiges can still be seen today, ensued between the merchant fleets of Portugal and the Netherlands. Portugal eventually lost its import monopoly from the Orient to the Dutch and to the commercial power of England, who now set foot in Asia and rapidly gained ground.

In 1755 an earthquake destroyed Lisbon and led to a great wave of reconstruction. The palace of Quelas was rebuilt and the king commissioned armorial table services in porcelain for his court receptions. The great families followed suit and orders flowed into China. The fashion for armorial services spread through Europe and the various Indies companies fulfilled the orders.

In 1602 and 1604 the Dutch captured two Portuguese carracks. Their cargoes, consisting of Chinese porcelain wares, were sold at auction in Amsterdam. This was the blue-and-white which became all the rage in Europe under the name of *Kraakporzellan* (carrack porcelain). Later this term served to describe all the blue-and-white porcelain, of very variable quality, which was produced for export from the mid-sixteenth century and throughout the seventeenth century. Although porcelain was originally confined to collectors, it soon found a wider market for everyday domestic use.

## NETHERLANDS

The route of Vasco de Gama, which might be called the Porcelain Route, became a scene of conflict and even pitched battles. The Portuguese and the Spanish defended it, and Dutch merchants had to resort to violence to break a way through to China.

Whereas in the Iberian peninsula the state possessed the means to assume the necessary military defence to protect its economic activities, the Dutch government, short of funds, was unable to invest in distant, risky expeditions.

The shipowners and merchants of the city-ports, who had capital available, therefore founded a company. Following the medieval tradition of corporations, the company demanded official confirmation of its statutes and monopoly privileges. Thus, with government support, the Dutch East India Company came into being.

The Dutch possessed ships built for trade and, if need be, for war; and it was with a fleet of eleven vessels that they set sail to establish their factories in Asia.

The Vereenigde Oostindische Compagnie (VOC) duly set up trading posts at the Cape, in Ceylon and in the Sunda Islands. On one of the islands, Java, it built a fortified town which served as the company's administrative centre. Batavia, today Jakarta, rapidly grew into an important international market which attracted all the buyers and sellers of South-east Asia. On the route to Japan, Batavia was also the supply base for the majority of ships embarked on this three-month-long voyage. Wealthy and powerful, the town enjoyed virtual political and economic independence.

The colonies of the Dutch East India Company flourished, and its network of commerce was well organised and highly efficient. Entire cargoes of porcelain arrived at Amsterdam and everything was immediately sold at auction. Buyers came from England, from Germany, from France and even more distant lands. Throughout the seventeenth century, profits were enormous, often paying shareholders 50 per cent or even 75 per cent dividends.

Europe was flooded with porcelain. In 1612 one ship brought 38,640 pieces to Amsterdam and in 1614 another

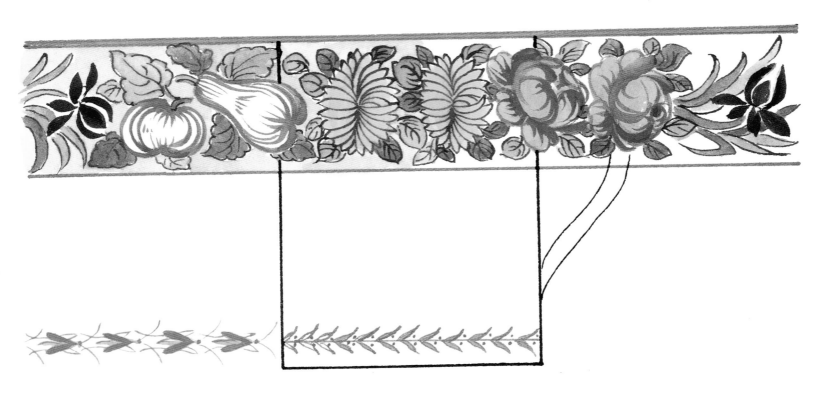

unloaded 69,057 pieces. According to estimates, the Dutch imported, between 1604 and 1656, more than three million pieces of porcelain.

Blue-and-white was greatly to Western taste and the porcelain blended perfectly with domestic interiors, introducing a note of fantasy and exoticism. Dutch painters immediately appreciated it for its decorative value and from the seventeenth century made it a feature of their still-lifes. Chinese porcelain rapidly conquered Europe.

Initially, it was selected on the basis of quality. These beautiful Chinese pieces compelled admiration and soon found eager art-lovers and collectors. When trade with the Far East intensified, porcelain became more accessible. Collecting was suddenly fashionable. At first there was less concern for quality than for sheer quantity and size, as for example in the case of mantelpiece ornaments. Most of the great art collections of Europe included a generous selection of porcelain, and private collectors kept theirs in special porcelain cabinets.

At the beginning of the eighteenth century the Oriental trade switched its interest to the utilitarian role of porcelain, turning out services or individual pieces made to order for clients. Commissions would be placed for a model in faience, tin, silver or even wood, and the design, in the form of an engraving or drawing, would be dispatched to the Far East for execution. The Chinese and Japanese managed to make faithful copies of these objects and themes, most of which were wholly alien to their culture.

During the eighteenth century the booming activity of the VOC and its power were badly shaken by native uprisings. The company finally disappeared at the same time as the downfall of the old republic (United Provinces) under the impact of the French Revolution.

## GREAT BRITAIN

The trading companies were private shareholding societies, constituted between the seventeenth and nineteenth centuries under the patronage and control of European states in order to exploit the wealth of overseas countries. They enjoyed a commercial monopoly and were protected by a national flag.

In England, a corporation of 'merchant adventurers' had, since 1556, specialised in exploring commercial relations with Muscovy (the Muscovy Company). In 1600 the first East India Company was founded, in 1661 the Africa Company (spices and tropical products), and in 1670 the Hudson's Bay Company (furs).

So long as the Portuguese and the French controlled the sea routes, the English East India Company had to be

▦ Jardinière inspired by a wine cooler made in China for the Dutch East Indies Company and destined for the English market.
Design by D. Alexiev

content with a fairly modest volume of trade. From 1699, however, the situation was completely reversed. The emperor Kangxi, wishing to expand commerce, opened Canton to the Europeans. Very soon companies from Denmark, Sweden, Austria and Spain established factories there. But the English East India Company proved so influential that English became the official language for all international transactions.

The East India Company grew so rapidly that it occupied the Indian province of Bengal and became a land power in its own right. The English government sent out a council and a court of justice to control its activities in the Indies. The governor general continued to conduct local policies and eventually the company extended its possessions to the entire Indian peninsula. In the nineteenth century, following uprisings, the British government wound up the East India Company and India became a crown colony.

Exploration and discovery had introduced new commodities which rapidly attracted a vast clientele. Luxuries such as Chinese tea, coffee and chocolate became everyday necessities in many households. Hundreds of thousands of porcelain dinner services were ordered and constituted the major part of ships' cargoes. In the eighteenth century England was the principal importer of such wares.

## FRANCE

While Portugal and the Netherlands cornered the lucrative trade with Asia, France was very slow to progress in that direction. French businessmen were not greatly attracted by the lure of distant adventure. It was Richelieu, and later Colbert, who took the first steps towards making France a great maritime and colonial power.

Several companies were created, all of them short-lived. Only one, Sieur Joudan du Groué's China Company, managed to send a ship to China. After setting up the first French factory at Canton in 1698, *L'Amphitrite* returned with a large cargo of porcelain. It was sold at auction, but soon the financial difficulties of the company put a halt to its activities.

Finally, in 1718, the French East India Company was founded to initiate and develop regular trade. As more and more cargoes arrived, porcelain soon became affordable. Whereas until the end of the seventeenth century services had been confined to the court, a handful of shipowners and a few noble families, such wares were now accessible to many people of means. The commissioned armorial service was proudly displayed on the dinner table of virtually all great families in the eighteenth century.

In France, as in the whole of western Europe, ordering porcelain from China was normal procedure. This overseas demand created a new branch of Chinese ceramics, known as 'commissioned' porcelain. Chinese artists succeeded in making very faithful imitations of pieces from Rouen, Nevers and Lille, in painting subjects inspired by Poussin, Mignard and the like, and in handling courtly and religious themes with equal facility.

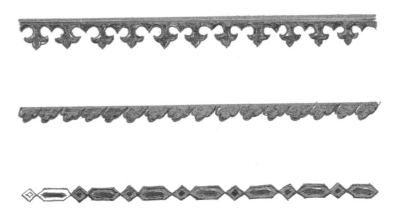

# Armorial Wares

■ Armorial plates
Design by R. Van der Broek and J. Fournier

Coats of arms or armorial bearings are coloured and patterned emblems of personal recognition, usually hereditary, granted to an individual, a family or a community, as defined and regulated by the science of heraldry. Those that appeared in Europe in the twelfth century responded to military needs. The insignia borne on shields served as the only means of identifying the knights to whom they once belonged.

Distinctive insignia of this nature went back, in fact, to ancient times. The Egyptians, the Greeks and the Romans all used figures and inscriptions as methods of identification in battle. And in countries far distant from the Mediterranean region, as in China, banners were employed not only for distinguishing the different elements of the army but also for conveying orders and directing manoeuvres on the battlefield.

In his preface to *The Art of War* by Sun Tzu, Samuel B. Griffith notes that the armies mentioned by Sun Tzu were composed of tactical elements capable of manoeuvring in an independent, coordinated fashion, and that battlefield orders were transmitted by trumpets, drums, flags and banners. Moreover, during the period of the Warring Kingdoms, a Chinese army drawn up in battle order would make an impressive sight, with its compact formations lined up and a multitude of standards and banners flapping in the breeze, the flags richly brocaded and adorned with figures of tigers, birds, dragons, serpents, phoenixes and tortoises, representing the staffs of the generals and those of the lieutenants commanding the flanks.

The above-mentioned insignia were collective emblems. Individual combat also entailed the use of particular signs, as was the case with the Greek warrior. After a long eclipse, in the twelfth century this reassumed importance in the guise of the medieval knight, who needed insignia in order to be identified. His horse and his armour, likewise signs of wealth and power, bore them also. The coats of arms which now appeared were painted, embroidered or woven on to the shield, the tunic, the helmet, the banners and the streamers.

The term 'coat of arms' derives from the coat or tunic which a man wore over his armour. Later it came to be applied specifically to the heraldic signs that appeared on the fighting man's shield. All the colours and patterns traditionally employed have their own descriptive terms (divisions, ordinaries and subordinaries) that make up the grammar of heraldry.

Heraldic charges originally included stylised animal figures such as the eagle, the lion, the unicorn or the dragon, but were in due course extended to other subjects, often defining status or profession, and including flowers, leaves, stars, coronets, weapons and abstract symbols. Crests, normally restricted to royalty and nobility, were often worn on the helmet, and various slogans and devices were also inscribed on streamers used, for example, by heralds announcing the entry of knights into the lists. The figures that stood on either side of the shield, consisting of a real or imaginary animal, were known as supporters.

The personal insignia of the nobility were hereditary to his family and descendants.

In the thirteenth century armorial bearings were increasingly employed. They appeared on the seals of bishoprics, clerks, distinguished citizens and towns. Later, in the fourteenth century, they were extended to abbeys and city corporations.

In France, to swell the funds of the royal treasury, Louis XIV, by an edict of 1696, established an armorial book in which heraldic arms were to be officially registered. This was the occasion for a large number of commoners to assume coats of arms as a right rather than a privilege. Abolished in 1790, armorial bearings were re-established by Napoleon, but only for the imperial nobility.

In eighteenth-century Europe there was a great demand for armorial dinner services. The various India Companies had them painted in China or Japan and supplied them in large quantities. Indeed, most of the 'commissioned' porcelain shipped to Europe consisted of these elaborate services.

Today these pieces, often exhibited in museums or stately homes, are there for all to admire. The colours of the *famille rose* wares are of incomparable freshness and beauty, and they are exquisitely made. The odd fault of orthography that slips into the device or Chinese head that appears by error in place of a helmet merely adds to their charm.

Armorial plates and other pieces are extremely decorative and continue to be made for special occasions and are often reproduced. It is essential to follow the model down to the last detail. Everything is codified and has a particular meaning: heraldry, after all, is a science.

Gold and silver are often used for armorial ware. Because of the expense involved in buying a single piece or simply because an alternative may be preferred, they can be replaced by metallic colours. But for those ambitious enough to make the attempt to decorate an armorial service, it is worthwhile obtaining matt gold or platinum, which are richer, not too ostentatious and more solid.

# *Historical Background*

■ Service inspired by *sometsuke* motifs. All the plates are different.
Design by Y. Alexiev

The advanced technology of Japan is a twentieth-century phenomenon that compels admiration. In past centuries, too, the West was captivated by the art of this distant and mysterious land. In the field of ceramics, Japan has made a significant contribution, and its development over the centuries can be better appreciated, as in the case of China, by knowledge of the key events and trends in the country's past.

The chain of islands that makes up Japan is an extreme prolongation of the continent of Asia. The insularity and isolation of Japan has played a major role in its history and culture. The country's physical structure and climate have likewise influenced the character and art of the population. The mountainous islands of Japan have very steep and picturesque coastlines. At the meeting point of the southerly monsoons and the northerly winds, of a tropical ocean current and a polar ocean current, Japan has an extraordinary and magnificent cover of vegetation. The many rivers and streams, the lakes and waterfalls, add beauty to the landscape. This natural beauty, to which the Japanese have always been sensitive, has played a important part both in their life and their art.

## JOMON PERIOD

The first manifestation of native artistic expression was in the field of ceramics. The earliest pottery was heavy, modelled by hand, yet distinguished by a formal variety and sculptural quality, and by imaginative abstract designs. This, the most ancient culture of Japan, began in the third millennium and flourished for over two thousand years. It is known by the name of Jomon (literally 'coiled'), its black pottery being decorated with impressions of coiled rope or matting. In this fashion the Jomon craftsmen made earthenware figurines known as *dogu*, which may have represented the Earth Mother, as well as 'medicine dolls' designed to attract the evil spirits responsible for illness.

Around the third century BC ethnic groups of the Mongol type arrived from the mainland, bringing with them a civilisation that had been influenced by China. They introduced rice cultivation and metalworking in bronze and iron.

From this, the Yayoi period (300 BC–AD300), contacts with continental Asia began. Various techniques were learned from Korea, including the use of the potter's wheel, to produce pieces of regular form typical of the ceramics of the Far East. More than 10,000 objects representing this civilisation have been retrieved from the great funerary mounds raised during this so-called 'antique sepulchres' period. Inserted in the ground encircling the mounds, the *haniwa*, covered with earth, served as decoration and as a magic barrier against evil spirits. The *haniwa* was originally a simple hollow pottery cylinder, pierced with holes and incisions, but the potter's art transformed these into statuettes representing animals and, more especially, men and women playing music, singing and dancing. They were clumsy, naive pieces, yet still extremely expressive.

From the third century BC, increasing contacts with Korea and China proved of capital importance to Japan's development. At the beginning of the fourth century entire colonies of Korean refugees, as well as Chinese families, settled in Japan bringing with them new techniques and trades such as weaving, embroidery and silkworm breeding. The cultural impact was considerable. Chinese language and writing were adopted to facilitate access to Chinese culture.

In the fifth century a new type of fine grey earthenware pottery, with a dense, hard grain appeared. This was stoneware, but it was not until the eighth century that the techniques of glazing were imported from China.

## ASUKA PERIOD (538–645)

Japan had no fixed capital. In order not to remain in a place marked by the death of an emperor, the seat of court moved around. In the early sixth century the court was installed at Asuka and this name served to describe the era. It coincided with the introduction of Buddhism and the overwhelming influence of China on the development of Japan.

In 538 the king of Paekche (Korea) sent to the emperor of Japan a bronze statue of Sakyamuni, urging him to embrace the Law of Buddha. It was Buddhism transformed in China, influenced by Taoist aspirations and harmony between man and nature. Japanese Shinto, with its worship of the forces of nature, showed the same tendencies. Buddhism spread rapidly and the two religions flourished side by side in a kind of symbiosis. In 587 it became the state religion, and henceforward the civilisation of China – writing, philosophy, political institutions and arts – permeated Japan.

Many Japanese decided to study the new religion in China. A succession of official missions, consisting of scholars, priests and artists, visited the country. They all returned impressed by this vast and powerful empire, its efficient organisation and the wealth of its cosmopolitan cities. In fact, China was embarking on one of the most splendid periods in history, the T'ang dynasty, and its prestige was enormous. In this climate of admiration, in order to acquire knowledge as rapidly as possible, the Japanese sent embassies consisting of hundreds of people, astonishingly eager to assimilate foreign culture.

Enthusiasm for the new faith gave a prodigious spur to architecture and sculpture. In the field of arts, the Japanese copied or derived inspiration from continental models. The impact of the T'ang era on Japanese art was so strong that it continues to this day to inspire artists, either directly or transmitted with modifications. However, the characteristic qualities of Japanese art also began to take shape: the sense of design, the elegance and refinement, the finish of the workmanship.

## NARA PERIOD (710–84)

Until now, without a permanent capital, Japan possessed no large towns. Highly impressed by Ch'ang-an, the magnificent T'ang capital, the Japanese decided to build one as well. In 710 the court was transferred to Nara which became the first capital of Japan and the first city built to a plan, the chessboard plan of Chinese towns. Within this convenient layout, many workshops devoted

■ Motifs based on the *Tale of Genji*. The subjects of this period are very decorative. Simplified and slightly enlarged, they can easily be adapted and interpreted on porcelain.

Screens are also an endless source of motifs. Even when simplified, they make a fine decorative effect. The gold grounds can be replaced by an ochre yellow and it is not even necessary to heighten them with gold.

The subject representing the young women among trees is taken from the *Tale of Genji*, but greatly simplified

## HEIAN PERIOD (794–1185)

Heian-Kyo, 'capital of peace and tranquillity', present-day Kyoto, succeeded Nara in 794 as capital of the Japanese empire. This geographical transfer was accompanied by a political and cultural upheaval. At this time, in China, the T'ang empire collapsed; diplomatic difficulties with Japan culminated in a break in 894. Relations with Korea, too, became hostile. Thus Japan went through several centuries of isolation and it was during this period of recession that the nation acquired its identity.

As far as the arts were concerned, towards the end of the Nara age, Japanese artists, having assimilated mainland culture, were already abandoning pure and simple imitation of Chinese models. This trend was to engender a specific art in which a taste for simplicity and conciseness, and above all a love of nature, were the dom-

to weaving, painting and lacquer, as well as bronze foundries, operated under the control and direction of the state treasury and were extraordinarily productive. So perfectly did they reproduce Chinese models that it is often difficult, even for experts, to distinguish objects made in China from those manufactured some years later in Japan.

inating features. It was a return to sources. In fact, nature played an active role in Japanese everyday life. It had been held sacred since time immemorial, and Shinto, the primitive religion of Japan, was a mixture of ancestor and nature worship, peopled by beneficent supernatural spirits (*kami*) who lived in animals, trees, rivers and mountains. From the Heian period, nature – until then utilised merely as an element of decoration – became an independent theme. The Japanese considered that it embodied the very essence of beauty and it was present in all branches of art.

In politics, the emperor eventually lost all authority and the country was governed by clans who disputed power. The first great family to play a key role in this struggle was that of the Fujiwara. The court remained the focal point of cultural life; divested of political power, it concentrated all its interest on the arts. Over the centuries it encouraged a style of life full of elegance and refinement. Works of art reflected this court culture, dedicated to beauty and perfection of form, to delicacy and poetry in relationships and feelings. This universe was described in all its detail in *The Tale of Genji* (*Genji monogatari*). The celebrated work by Murasaki Shikibu is representative of the courtly romances of the age.

Fascinated by writing and poetry, the Japanese had built up a body of national literature which duly provided subjects for painters. The visual interpretation of literary works led to painting that was wholly secular and purely Japanese in style. The small pictures that illustrate poems and courtly romances convey states of mind rather than describing actions and events. Yet the facial expressions reveal no hint of feeling, for the features are schematised to the extreme: the eye is indicated by a stroke and the nose by a hook.

The faces are without tone and the emotions felt by the persons portrayed are suggested only by the colours employed and the atmosphere emanating from the composition.

Nature, with its blossoming trees and grass swaying in the autumn wind, with its melancholy moon or cloudless sky, reflects the links between people and their feelings.

Another form of illustration (*e-makimono*) was employed in the *Legends of Mount Shigi* (*Shigi-san engi*). Painted on long horizontal scrolls, the pictures describe a sequence of events.

Leisurely examination of them conveys an impression of time and space. In this dynamic, almost cinematographic, style of painting the faces are full of life. It may be deduced that the people represented are not noble. This contrast between the aristocracy and the common folk was already underlined in the statues of protohistory.

Rivalry among clans gave rise to a warrior caste, that of the *samurai*, who made up the private armies. Even Buddhism, in spite of its pacifist principles, found itself involved in the violence of the age.

The monks of Mount Hiei had their own priorities and their army of mercenaries terrorised the capital. Japan was to know three centuries of troubles and bloody, destructive civil wars.

### KAMAKURA (1185–1332), NAMBOKUCHO (1333–91) AND MUROMACHI (1392–1572) PERIODS

The Minamoto clan finally emerged victorious, leaving the emperor his title and representative role. Yoritomo, chief of the clan, established his headquarters at Kamakura and this parallel capital gave its name to the period. He aimed to keep his warriors and officials far from the court, with its frivolity and intrigues. Nevertheless, many capable people left Kyoto to work in the new administration, bringing with them a taste for art and culture which helped to change the atmosphere of this military dictatorship. So, when peace was reestablished, orders were given for the restoration of monuments damaged by the civil war, providing fresh impetus for the arts.

At the same time that Japan emerged from its phase of isolation there was a resumption of scientific and cultural exchanges. China once more exerted strong influence on local art. Japanese Zen monks were inspired by Chinese temples. Zen, a sect known as Ch'an in China, was introduced during the Kamakura period and became very powerful.

The Zen influence on art was considerable, even in unusual fields such as gardening and the tea ceremony. The sect demanded strict discipline and frugality, and this austerity is well illustrated by the economy of elements making up the 'dry gardens' that appeared in the Muromachi period. Composed of gravel paths meticulously raked every day and symbolising water, and 'islands' of stone representing universal order, these gardens were conceived to encourage meditation and acquisition of knowledge through manual activities.

This period ended with two attempted invasions of Japan by the Mongols of Kublai Khan, who had conquered China in 1260, and then Korea and Indochina. The Japanese repulsed the Mongols but the Kamakura leaders emerged much weakened. Civil war broke out again and lasted more than fifty years (the Nambokucho period). In 1392 Ashikaga Takauji proclaimed himself shogun and assumed the reins of government in place of the emperor. The palace of the Ashikaga shoguns was situated in the Muromachi district of Kyoto, hence the name given to this era.

Despite the incessant conflicts, there remained a constant interest in literature and the arts. They were not exclusively the province of the court: the Ashikaga shoguns were generous patrons. On the other hand, the Zen monks were the self-appointed masters of knowledge and culture. First they established contacts with the Chinese branch of the sect; then official relations recommenced with China. In 1543 Portuguese merchants were the first Europeans to reach Japan. Three years later they were followed by a group of Jesuit missionaries led by St Francis Xavier. Received with goodwill, Christianity found disciples and developed apace, but its relationship with the authorities remained confused. It became embroiled in political intrigue and eventually fell prey to terrible persecution.

The Muromachi period was favourable to trade, and in spite of the pirates who roamed the coasts of China, commercial traffic was heavy. The merchant class that sprang up in Japan assumed great importance and stimulated the arts with its patronage. Works of art occupied pride of place in commercial exchanges with China. The Japanese exported paper, lacquer and bronzes against silk, books and porcelain. Chinese influence was strongly felt in all areas.

The Zen monks were greatly attracted by monochrome painting in ink and the sober, expressive style that the Chinese masters of the Song era had inherited from the scholars of the T'ang dynasty. This style harmonised perfectly with Japanese sensibility. In Japan, where communion with nature is a source of happiness and inspiration, it attains its apogee in the field of landscape. The latent nostalgia that one senses in these wash

Sesshu (1420–1506) had a powerful, expressive and inventive touch. This interpretation of one of his landscapes cannot possibly reproduce his strength and originality

drawings reveals a certain sadness tinged with passion and violence, perhaps buried deep in the Japanese soul. Painters such as Sesshu, unequalled in power and originality, surpassed their masters of the Ming era.

Yet painting in the traditional Japanese style, highly decorative and colourful, did not disappear. It was continued by the school of Tosa which worked for the imperial court, while the painters of the Kano family, who

The coats of arms (*mon*) of Nobunaga, Hideyoshi and Ieyasu in black and gold. The *mon* or family escutcheon is often represented on the sleeve of the clothing. These coats of arms, stylised and beautifully designed, are employed as decorative motifs. A single *mon* is enough to cover the lid of a small box. Several of them, in groups or scattered harmoniously over the surface of a large piece, constitute a dignified and elegant pattern which blends with domestic interiors

that the Chinese jealously guarded the secret of porcelain manufacture from foreigners. Thus, although perfected at home in the middle years of the T'ang period (618–906), it was some five centuries before true porcelain appeared in Korea, which actually formed part of the Chinese peninsula.

It was produced in Japan two centuries later by Gorodayu Shonzui, who, by 1510, had spent some five years in Jingdezhen, the centre of the Chinese porcelain industry, and returned home with all the necessary materials. Having settled near Arita, a town in the Hizen region of the island of Kyushu, he made porcelain decorated in underglaze blue until his death in 1550. These facts are sustained mainly by legend, for the document relating them is unreliable and no single piece of his production has so far come to light. True or not, it was in the Hizen region that ceramics production was intensified after the Nambokucho and Muromachi periods.

## MOMOYAMA PERIOD (1573–1602)

The Ashikaga shoguns proved incapable of governing this land where war was endemic. They were ousted by Oda Nobunaga, a petty *daimyo* (hereditary prince) who had managed to conquer a large part of central Japan. He was a very violent, cruel man, even by contemporary Japanese standards. He crushed his rivals and proceeded to subjugate the military provincial governors, who had set themselves up as *daimyo*, as well as the warrior monks of Mount Hiei and other fortified monasteries. Victim of a conspiracy in 1584, he was replaced by one of his generals. Toyotomi Hideyoshi (1536–98) finally succeeded in unifying and pacifying a nation that had been tearing itself apart for centuries. A man of immense ambition and vision, he is regarded as one of the major figures of Japanese history. Commanding an army of 250,000 men, he envisaged conquering China where the power of the Ming dynasty was in decline. First he attacked Korea but his two expeditions, in 1592 and 1598, were disasters and his death put a halt to the venture.

Whereas commerce during the Muromachi era had contributed to the development of the urban population and encouraged the growth of a merchant class, the incessant wars had promoted the fortunes of the professional warriors. Having distinguished themselves by their courage and military ability, these men of modest origins eventually succeeded to the highest office. This

directed the shogun's workshop, retained the decorative character of painting yet added a new note by adopting monochrome. These painters went on to reconcile ink and colour in art, thus creating a new and typically Japanese style.

The Japanese produced traditional pottery and stoneware, some of which, finding beauty in simplicity and naturalism, was used for tea ceremonies. However, the Japanese had always been entranced by Chinese ceramics, especially during the Song era when stoneware and porcelain reached the apex of perfection. The Japanese were very late to enter this field but the truth is was a new phenomenon in Japanese society where such functions had long been hereditary. The new military administration imposed order and strict discipline and mercilessly punished the smallest insubordination.

These dignitaries were soon rivalling the ancient families in their refined lifestyle and appreciation of the arts. They built enormous castles, decorated them in a luxurious style and opened them up to poets and artists who converted them into centres of culture. The name given to this era is derived from the castle of Momoyama, which was built for Hideyoshi and where he surrounded himself with writers and scholars.

Art evolved from the sacred to the secular, adorning private homes rather than temples, monasteries and shrines. The finest artists were called in to decorate castle interiors which reflected the wealth and power of their owners. Wall paintings and movable screens were essential elements in the decoration of these luxurious dwellings. Sobriety was replaced by a taste for magnificence, the austerity of wash gave way to an explosion of colour, a widespread use of gold and an abundance of detail in decoration. Minor decorative arts such as lacquerwork, costume design for the *no* theatre, and textile manufacture, reached unprecedented levels.

The art of textile design was greatly encouraged in Japan. During the Heian period, an age of refined aestheticism, feminine court costume comprised a dozen or so robes on top of one another, and dressing was an art in itself. This interest in clothing was a spur to creativity, embodied in painted, embroidered and brocaded materials or in a combination of techniques in which the designs were often done by unknown artists. Even though over the centuries the style became simplified, nonetheless it retained its character of opulence. The kimono, for example, was basically of a very simple cut, yet it required extraordinary effect because of its patterns and its skilfully harmonised or contrasted colours. Textile designers and weavers were, and still are, highly esteemed artists. Hideyoshi, who protected and encouraged the arts, summoned back to Kyoto many weavers who had fled the city, settling them in the Nishijin quarter which thereafter maintained its supremacy in the field of silk weaving. Kimonos and Japanese textiles constitute a limitless source of ideas for decorative porcelain painting.

The end of the Momoyama period marked a turning point in ceramics production. During the retreat of Hideyoshi's armies, a number of potters were brought back from Korea as prisoners or immigrants. Their flourishing activity gave new impetus to the manufacture of pottery and traditional stoneware. Some ceramics, such as those of Karatsu, were so influential that they came to be known as 'Korean karatsu'. Tanaka Chojiro, the son of one of these potters, was the first to make in his workshop at Kyoto, *raku* porcelain, which is still manufactured today. This ware, like that of Karatsu, owes its fame to the tea ceremony, introduced by the Zen monks. The ritual took place in a small rustic pavilion that formed part of a simple, quiet garden given over to meditation.

The code of beauty of the 'tea masters' was simplicity above all else, and both the decoration and the utensils were conceived in this spirit. The tea bowls were unique pieces, irregular and unpolished, their decoration confined to a layer of glaze, a natural effect of the material or, more rarely, a barely suggested motif.

Another of these craftsmen, Lee Champyong, known by the name of Ri Sampei (Ree San-Pei) in Japan, was brought from the Korean countryside by the *daimyo* Nabeshima Naoshige, who settled him on his own land in the Hizen region. According to tradition, Ri Sampei was the first porcelain manufacturer in Japan, attributed with the discovery, in 1616, not far from the town of Arita, of a large deposit of kaolin, which is still being worked today. Ri Sampei did indeed exist and excavations have revealed that he did in fact manufacture utilitarian blue-and-white porcelain of somewhat mediocre quality.

## TOKUGAWA PERIOD (1603–1867)

Tokugawa Ieyasu, one of Hideyoshi's rivals, seized power on the latter's death, becoming shogun in 1603. He chose to govern from his own lands on the island of Honshu; and his capital, Edo (present-day Tokyo) gave its name to the entire period.

The first concern of Tokugawa Ieyasu was to make his power unassailable. He eliminated the Hideyoshi family for good by capturing their fortress of Osaka. Then, in order to weaken his feudal lords, he stripped them of their wealth and proceeded to redistribute their holdings to his followers. These new *daimyo* were also kept under control and were obliged every year to appear at court, at their own expense, or to leave family hostages there. The peasants lived in abject misery and were likewise kept under close surveillance: each group of five families represented a unit, placed under the responsibility of elders. Finally, the emperor and his court were denied any participation in state affairs and had no contact with the outside world.

Ieyasu also feared the influence of foreign missionaries and of Christian doctrine, which he forbade in 1615. The missionaries were compelled to leave the country and native Christians were cruelly persecuted. Any form of uprising was crushed pitilessly. The peasant uprising of Shimabara (1637–8), vaguely inspired by Christian ideals but even more by economic hardships, culminated in a massacre of unprecedented proportions. In 1640, all foreigners were expelled and the Japanese were forbidden, on pain of death, to leave the country. The closure of Japan was complete and was to last for two centuries.

The measures against foreigners were nevertheless subject to exceptions in the case of the Chinese and, more particularly, the Dutch. The Dutch East India Company had established a number of factories in Asia, including one at Hirado (1609). The reason why the Dutch were favoured was, above all, because they restricted themselves to matters of trade without meddling in Japanese internal affairs. Even so, they were requested to leave Hirado and to rebuild their factory on the small artificial island of Deshima, opposite Nagasaki. There they were kept under supervision, being unable to leave the island without authorisation.

Until that time the Dutch had not exported Japanese porcelain, trading only in Chinese products. In 1644 civil war broke out, toppling the Ming dynasty and paralysing the whole of China. Not only were industries ransacked and destroyed, but the rebels imposed a blockade of the southern coast of China, virtually halting all commercial activity. The Dutch East India Company exported practically no more Chinese porcelain between 1657 and 1681, switching its interest towards the newer Japanese porcelain which imitated Chinese blue-and-white. It urged the Japanese to copy these models as precisely as possible and to step up production. This stimulating combination of circumstances proved decisive for porcelain manufacture in Japan and exports rocketed.

After the difficult period which served to consolidate their power, the Tokugawa imposed and maintained peace until the mid-nineteenth century. The regime encouraged the installation of local ceramics, lacquer and textile factories in all regions, even in those areas that did not thus far possess a tradition of craftsmanship. The towns grew, inland trade increased and industries developed. The commercial class, already flourishing in the Muromachi period, made steady progress, becoming the most prosperous social category in Japan and playing a key role in cultural life.

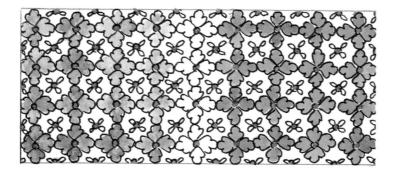

▨ Right: Ancient Kakiemon motifs of the 'Korean' type

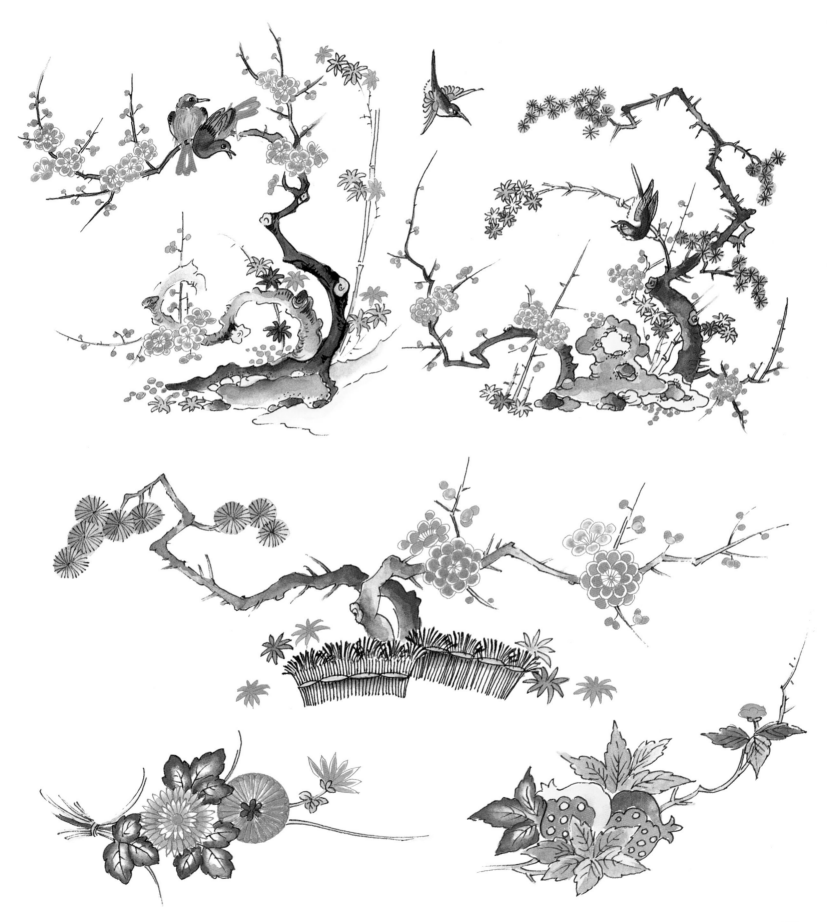

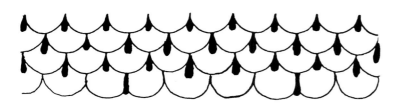

In this atmosphere of isolation, under strict army and police rule, special privileges were conferred upon the military aristocracy which governed the country. During their obligatory stays at Edo, the *daimyo* focused their interest on luxury, pleasure and the arts. Decoration in all forms was the vogue, and even the major arts followed this trend.

One form of art that made prodigious strides in the Tokugawa period was wood engraving. This procedure, making it possible to take a large number of copies of a single original work, developed so as to incorporate painting. The increasingly prosperous urban population sought to adorn their homes and the acquisition of prints suited such a need perfectly. Great Japanese artists turned to this field and, when their work became known in Europe, influenced the Impressionists and the decorative arts.

One of the first masters of the polychrome print, Suzuki Harunobu, elaborated the ideal type of feminine beauty: a slim, supple body, full of grace and elegance, tiny hands and feet, and a fine head of hair. The faces remained as

empty of expression as those of *The Tale of Genji*. These beauties, dressed in splendid kimonos, attended to their make-up, strolled and relaxed in an architectural or natural setting.

The prints are a marvellous subject source for porcelain and are easy to reproduce. The motifs that represent people are highly decorative and it is possible to find models in the work of the great artists, of whom Torii Kiyonaga and, above all, Kitagawa Utamaro (1753–1806) worthily celebrated Japanese womanhood. For anyone interested in nature and landscapes, the best models are the prints of Katsushika Hokusai (1760–1849) and Ando Hiroshige (1797–1858). It is often possible to take one part of a work, adapting, simplifying or changing the colours, but the essential consideration is that the whole composition should be harmonious and in the spirit of Japanese aesthetics.

This applies to the decoration of the vase on the facing page, inspired by a print of Nishikawa Sukenobu (1671–1751), in which the colours have been completely changed.

Despite its isolation, Japan continued to be pervaded by foreign influences. In the two main currents of Japanese painting, we find the influence of individual, impressionistic research as well as that of the academic, meticulous style of the schools of northern and southern China. Moreover, the presence of the small Dutch colony permitted a contact, certainly limited, but which brought in a great deal of information about the West. The Japanese discovered, from prints of scientific works, the naturalism of Western art and were very intrigued by the faithful representation of nature – a concept that was alien to them.

Japanese painting, in fact, sought to express the spirit and essence of subjects rather than to represent them realistically. Some painters were tempted by this genre and briefly introduced more realism into their works.

Of all the arts, it was ceramics which was most in touch with the outside world. It adapted itself to the tastes of its clients in South-west Asia and even interpreted European subjects. However, the authentic Japanese inspiration was not lost and produced porcelain wares of incomparable quality. When they reached Europe, they were appreciated for their true worth and served as a model for the burgeoning porcelain industry there.

▓ Right: vase representing three young women
Design by N. Caramanis

Unfortunately, Japanese porcelain was too expensive. Passing through the hands of many intermediaries, its price increased beyond reason and its manufacture remained on a small scale. It could not compete with the Chinese porcelain industry when the latter resumed normal activity, and Japanese exports suffered a marked decline. On the other hand, Chinese potters were in their turn obliged to copy Japanese designs and glazes.

The Tokugawa, who helped develop industry and commerce, showed themselves incapable of understanding and controlling economic problems. The peasants, exhausted by poor crops and conditions of misery, rose in revolt, local lords fell into debt and the later Tokugawa heads of government lacked statesmanlike qualities and vision. The last shogun was forced to abdicate in 1867 and, emerging from the shadows, the Meiji emperor formed alliances with the nobles. The Western powers, steadily expanding their interests in the Far East, succeeded, through diplomacy and intimidation, in opening up the country. Japan was experiencing political, social and technological change, and the Meiji era, symbolically known as the 'enlightened government', transformed the feudal state into a modern state.

The vase on page 117 is done in several stages:
1  Transfer the enlarged subject to the piece.
2  Do the outlines, as well as the details, in violet and fix the drawing by firing.
3  Colour a part of the motif and fire.
4  Colour the remaining parts and fire.
5  Finish in gold and fire.

The firing of the drawing will not work if a sugar mixture is used. However, some prefer to fix it for working on large pieces and thus avoid the risk of obliteration by contact with damp hands.

Two firings are necessary when the colours that touch one another are applied by tinting. In this case, for the first firing, use dark colours. For the second, apply light colours and then carefully (without overflowing) deepen the dark colours as necessary.

It is also preferable to colour the motifs of the kimonos before or after the background colour of the materials. There is no risk of colours interfering with each other when one of them is fired.

Rocks, from which spring a flowering stem and a twisted tree, are inspired by Chinese motifs. The one represented in the illustration is based on fantasy, as in mainland models, but on porcelain of the Japanese Kakiemon style the rocks are more realistic. The reason is to be sought not only in the inherently Japanese sense of precision and simplification, but more especially in the love they feel for nature. Rocks, often present even in the smallest gardens, represent the mountains of this natural landscape which the Japanese try to reproduce in order to escape from their overcrowded cities.

Even a very simple subject will suffice for decoration provided the workmanship is good. The trees in the four corners of the illustration can decorate the centre of a pin-tray or the lid of a box: three of them can be put on the outer rims of a cup and one on the bottom. In the original model, they are in blue, but certain parts can be done in gold. However, care must be taken to retain the proportions of the composition.

Right: In centre, blue-and-white plate from the early eighteenth century: d. 25 cm
This illustration combines several classic themes of Oriental porcelain: the phoenix, the rock and the hedge
The phoenix (*ho-o* in Japanese), taken from Chinese models, is found on *sometsuke*, Imari and Kakiemon wares. It is the symbol of wisdom and energy

# Kyushu Porcelain

Nabeshima: plates with 'hedge' decoration and herons respectively
Design by F. Fournier and T. de Ternoy

Korean potters introduced porcelain to Japan. For the most part they made crockery: bowls, teacups, small plates and censers. The earliest designs were in the Korean style and done with a single firing, the blue being directly applied to the piece before glazing. Intended for a domestic market, this production was quite rare.

## BLUE-AND-WHITE

Chinese porcelain, long present in Japan, was highly valued and early Korean motifs gradually disappeared in favour of Chinese models. Chinese influence dominated the style of Japanese blue-and-white ware, production of which increased considerably. It was in fact a particularly auspicious time for this industry to develop. The growing demand for Chinese porcelain in Europe could not be satisfied because of the slowing down, almost the halting, of production following the disorders in China. Jingdezhen, paralysed by the civil war, could no longer fulfil orders, and the Japanese were invited to replace Chinese wares on the European market.

Ceramics was at this period a craft production in Japan and a major effort was needed to enlarge kilns, increase output and face overseas demand. The Dutch wanted copies of Chinese pieces and the Japanese managed to imitate them so successfully that certain products may be mistaken for Chinese blue-and-white.

As regards native Japanese blue-and-white ware, this differs in the concept of the decoration. Landscapes are typically Japanese with their waterfalls and little bridges; the designs are off-centre and asymmetric, and the motifs of geometrical regularity are characteristically precise.

It is not known whether the chrysanthemum also grew in Japan or whether it was introduced from Korea or from China at the beginning of the Christian era. In any event, it became, together with the prunus, the national flower of Japan and after the Kamakura period it was used in all the decorative arts.

## Blue and gold plate

The copy (facing page) is done in three stages:

1 Draw the peony branch and position the chrysanthemums very precisely.
   - Trace the peony motif with the pen in sugar mixture and then colour.
   - Tint the area of the chrysanthemums light blue.
   - Fire.
2 Draw the large chrysanthemum leaves in pencil, then colour tint in dark blue.
   - Paint the long stalks of grass behind the peonies with a decorating brush.
   - Retouch the peony branch.
   - Paint all the small leaves that fill the space occupied by the chrysanthemums with a medium brush in dark blue.
   - Fire.
3 Draw the chrysanthemums with the pen, using gold.
   - Paint with a decorating brush the outlines and veins of the large leaves, as well as the touches that mark the small background leaves.
   - Fire gold.

## IMARI

The ceramic industry was concentrated on the island of Kyushu, around Arita in Hizen province, where the Korean potters, brought in during the military expeditions to Korea, had founded a number of workshops. The region had two ports. At Imari, regional production was assembled and then transported to Nagazaki, where the Dutch East India Company's factory was located. In time, the name Imari came to be applied to the entire production of Arita and its neighbourhood, comprising the following groups:

1 Porcelain decorated in underglaze blue, called *sometsuke* (old Arita).
2 Porcelain copied from Chinese productions of Swatow (*gosu-aka-e*), decorated in underglaze blue, iron red and green enamels.
3 Polycrome porcelain, known as Imari.

In Japan the name Imari is given to all these porcelain wares – except those attributed to Kakiemon and Nabeshima – produced at Hirado. On the other hand, in Europe, Imari applies only to the porcelain with an underglaze blue design, completed after the first firing with motifs mainly in iron red and gold. Three types of European Imari are thus distinguished:

1 Decorated with three colours (*sancai*): underglaze blue, underglaze iron red and gold; this type of Imari was much copied by the Chinese, hence the name Chinese Imari.
2 Decorated with five colours (*gosai*): underglaze blue, iron red, violet or yellow enamels, or the two plus green and gold. The decoration of this porcelain is abundant and sometimes covers the whole surface; large white spaces punctuate the underglaze blue ground and are occupied by graceful motifs copied from Chinese models, but interpreted in the Japanese manner. This group of Imari is much appreciated in Japan.
3 Decorated in the 'brocaded style' (*nishiki-de*) the chromatic palette used is identical to that of five-colour Imari but differs in decoration, which entirely covers the surface of the piece. Underglaze blue spaces serve as a ground for a rich ornamentation in gold and the general effect is sumptuous. This style had great success in Europe during the Baroque era. It was employed for decorating show pieces such as mantelpiece ornaments, groups made up of three big-bellied vases with lids and groups of two straight vases with a wide lip and no lid.

The brocaded style was not considered by the Japanese to be very artistic, but they produced such ware in numbers to satisfy demand. In the second half of the

▨ The original version of this piece was a small saucer in underglaze blue (*sometsuke*) and gold from Arita, dating from the early seventeenth century. The asymmetric composition represents a branch of peony and grasses sprouting from a bunch of chrysanthemums: d. 18.5 cm
Design by A. Cassagne

eighteenth century they added underglaze black to the original palette and used it to create monumental or miniaturised pieces with even more overloaded decoration.

Meanwhile China, where in the late seventeenth century order had been restored and industry revived, profited from the success of Imari porcelain. At Jingdezhen, both the blue, red and gold and brocaded styles were copied and mass-produced. And in Europe, the first manufacturers of porcelain began successfully to imitate the Japanese products. These two factors resulted in the European market becoming saturated; and this coincided with changes in taste and fashion.

In 1828 Arita was ravaged by fire and manufacture of this type of porcelain practically ceased. European interest in Imari wares revived around 1860 and stimulated a new wave of production; also by this time modern technology was set to bring about a revolution. In the nineteenth century porcelain production in Japan entered the industrial age. Simplified designs, wholly in red-and-gold, date from this period. Broadly speaking, there was a fall in quality standards at the expense of quantity. Cheap Japanese porcelain flooded Europe and posed a grave threat to local production.

The large dish on the left was made in the following sequence:

1 Photocopying the document and enlarging to the size of the dish.
   - Transferring to the dish with tracing and carbon paper.
   - Drawing with pen.
   - Firing.
2 Colouring the flowers with a very light iron red; painting the branches and leaves dark blue.
   - Tinting the vase on the dish, the large leaves and the onions dark blue.
   - Colouring the bands blue.
   - Painting all the gold motifs on the white porcelain alone.
   - Firing.
3 Painting in gold all those parts of the work which bring out the detail of the painted blue motifs, i.e. vase, central trunk and branches, leaves of the flower composition, big leaves and onions on the wing.
   - Firing the gold.

▓ Chinese Imari dish of the Kangxi period, end of seventeenth century
Design by M.-F. Hendrix

The basket of flowers on the following page was the design of Lan Ts'ai, patron of florists and one of the Taoist Eight Immortals. It is the symbol of harmony, expressing a wish for agreement and good relations. The original motif is Chinese and generally represents a bamboo basket with flowers arranged in no particular order. In Japan it is a free adaptation as far as the receptacle is concerned, but the flower compositions are carefully done, often having symbolic meaning. Some of the motifs, done to the taste and demand of European clients, are notable for the symmetrical arrangement of the flowers.

These are some suggestions for using the motifs in question:

1 The flower vases can be used for decorating tall pieces (feet of lamp, vase, etc.). Enlarge the bouquet or stretch the branches a little, adding one or two flowers, to provide the height. Arrange the motif:
   a) in the middle of the belly if the vase is ovoid in shape;
   b) on one face, alternating it with one face tinted or reworked in gold (brocade style) if it is a vase with sides.
2 Use the different elements of decoration of the wing and central plate separately for boxes, pin-trays and other small objects.
3 By enlarging the two friezes at the base of the page, it is possible to get a complete motif for a teacup or coffee cup, for bowls or even for a large decorative band around a larger piece.

## KAKIEMON

Kakiemon porcelain represents a break with the Chinese style and its all-embracing, excessive ornamentation. It is distinctive for its wholly Japanese polychrome decoration. It was produced by the Sakaida family of ceramists who have transmitted their skills from father to son to this very day. The head of the firm had his kiln not far from Arita and manufactured *sometsuke*. Documents say that his son, Sakaida Kizaemon, had originally been a samurai of the *daimyo* of Nabeshima. However, around 1625 he had business connections with Higashijima Tokuzaemon, an important dealer of Imari who also had the job of supervising the entire porcelain production of Arita. The latter had bought glazing formulae from a Chinese potter living in Nagasaki and had transmitted them to Sakaida Kizaemon, asking him to try to produce this type of decoration in the family workshop, which duly turned out overglaze-decorated porcelain using polychrome enamels (*aka-e nishiki-de*). This new technique was not easy to develop, for the original information was somewhat vague and it was necessary to find suitable enamels from the materials available on the spot; it took twenty years for the Sakaida family to master it.

According to tradition, Kizaemon offered the *daimyo* of Nabeshima a decorative piece (*okimono*) representing two persimmons (*kaki*). This gift, decorated by means of the new technique, proved so acceptable that he conferred on Sakaida a new name, that of Kakiemon. From this time the elder sons of the family took over the workshop and bore the name Kakiemon. In another version, the name was chosen because of the resemblance of the orange-red glaze, characteristic of the decoration, to the colour of the *kaki*.

▓ The illustration on the left shows a motif often seen on Imari porcelain, that of flower-decorated vases, which in itself is very decorative. It is completed by two friezes of Imari plates
Above, right: Imari vase  Design by N. Caramanis

Kakiemon I decided, in order to keep the secrets of the glazing, only to transmit them to the holder of the name. So it was effectively guarded during the first three generations. Later, there were leaks, and the technique of enamel decoration was practised elsewhere; nevertheless, Kakiemon porcelain has always retained its individual and unmistakable style. The workshop was sometimes directed by less talented members of the family who just about managed to keep things going, and sometimes by more dedicated men who gave great impetus to production. Today the business run by Kakiemon XIV is prospering and its porcelain enjoys worldwide prestige.

Kakiemon porcelain is distinctive not only for its style of decoration but also for the remarkable quality of its paste and the elegance of its shape. Its whiteness is described as *nigoshide*, which means 'rice water', or as 'milky white'. On this very white ground the decorative motifs done with bright, luminous glazes stand out incomparably.

Kakiemon XIV, whilst conforming to tradition, creates designs full of presence and novelty. He borrows his subjects from the local flora, which he studies from nature, and then makes beautiful compositions according to the shape and size of the pieces.

These very attractive motifs are not as easy as they might seem. Their apparent simplicity demands much precision and perfect workmanship. Moreover, modern European glazes lack the transparency and reliability of those that show to such advantage on Kakiemon porcelain, and for that reason many prefer to use ordinary colours. The vase on page 131 is done with enamels, except for the red.

### Practical Advice:

The motifs represented on the plate are done by pen but on porcelain they should be done with a decorative brush. The adjoining leaf in black and white shows clearly how the brush drawing is done.
The leaves and the stems are in black but, for the drawing of the flowers and the pale yellow strawberries, use dark red or purple.

## NABESHIMA

The name of Nabeshima, already mentioned, is closely associated with Japanese porcelain. The *daimyo* of Nabeshima had brought potters from the Korean countryside to help develop the art of ceramics in his lands. The Nabeshima clan then ruled Arita and its neighbourhood. In 1628 the *daimyo* decided to build his private kiln and set up a workshop south of Arita. Later this was twice moved further away from the town with the aim of preserving the secret of the techniques employed. The craftsmen who worked there were not permitted to stray beyond a certain perimeter and anyone who who wished to be hired was obliged to accept these conditions. The workshop and the village were guarded; no visitor or businessman was admitted. All flawed pieces were destroyed instead of being given away so that the models should not be publicised and imitated.

Sakaida Kizaemon contributed greatly to the organisation and growth of the workshop. He was put in charge of it and introduced the production of high-quality celadons. It was he, according to another story, who bore the title Kakiemon I.

Initial production was of blue-and-white ware but very soon polychrome decoration was introduced. The motifs were designed in underglaze blue and the drawings were extremely painstaking and precise. Later they were painted with enamels in green, yellow and a special, characteristic red, darker than the orange-red of Kakiemon wares. Furthermore, their yellow was purer and their green more bluish.

The Nabeshima workshop aimed at quality and its production was exceptional. The porcelain was reserved exclusively for family use and for the gifts that the *daimyo* offered the shogun. Given these conditions, it was some time before it became known in Europe. This policy, however, was unprofitable and could not be pursued indefinitely, particularly when in the nineteenth century the Nabeshima clan found itself in an increasingly serious economic situation. Quality suffered and began to deteriorate.

When the Meiji government replaced the feudal system by a prefectorial administration, the

reorganisation, and in the second half of the century porcelain began to be mass-produced. Major changes of this nature necessitated equally drastic changes in form and design. Neo-classicism – its last phase reflected in the Empire style – began to disappear after 1820. It was a period of confused experiment. Around 1830 rococo made a come-back but soon collapsed from surfeit and exaggeration. Originating in France, the fashion enjoyed much popularity in England, but was received more cautiously in other countries. The artists imitated older models in the rococo style and there was a return to motifs inspired by Chinese and Japanese porcelain, and of *chinoiseries*. These were compara-tively easy to copy, and probably this was a consideration, but despite this advantage the revival was fairly modest.

The evolution of European art during the nineteenth century was strongly influenced by that of the Orient. In 1854 the Americans managed to open up trade between Japan and the nations of Europe.

▨ Motifs drawn from nineteenth-century Bayeux production
Design by M. Castel

While Japan benefited from this direct contact with the industrial discoveries of the West, Japanese art found its way into Europe. Its impact was enormous and instan-taneous, nowhere more so than in France and especially on the Impressionist painters.

Japanese art, now as in earlier periods, was directly inspired by nature. Based on first-hand observation, it depicted plants and animals in a style that was at once realistic and poetic, sometimes reduced to essential detail. The composition, often asymmetric, was simple and uncluttered, conveying the essence of the subject

and affording ample scope for the painter's talents. European artists studied these concepts, admired them and adopted them. Their encounter with Japanese art was a stimulus. Its inspiration, through adaptation, altered their own vision. Thus was born the phenomenon that came to be called Japanism.

Samuel Bing wrote on 1 May 1888 in the first number of his magazine *Artistic Japan*: 'This art [of the Far East] has long mingled with our own. It is like a drop of blood that has mingled with our blood and no power in the world can remove it.'

▨ Japanese vase with wisteria. The opening up of Japan also heralded a tidal wave of Japanese porcelain wares, which posed a threat to European production
This type of design, and particularly the representation of plants and animals in Japanese drawing and prints, was a determining factor in the introduction of Japanism
Design by M. Castel

# The Oriental Influence

■ Pot holder with gilded Delft decoration
Design by A. Cassagne

Although China was the cradle of porcelain manufacture, it was in the Middle East and specifically the countries dominated by Islam that the glazed earthenware known as faience was most widely produced. Introduced into Europe, where the arts of the Far East were greatly appreciated, it stimulated the imitation of Chinese wares and paved the way for the discovery of soft-paste porcelain.

## HOLLAND
### Delft

Holland, after Portugal, was in the seventeenth century the principal importer of ceramics from the Far East. Hence the Dutch manufacturers of faience were among the first to recognise the quality and worth of Oriental porcelain. The popularity of blue-and-white persuaded them to make copies of it to satisfy the growing numbers of collectors. At Delft a number of workshops were built, some of them on the sites of bankrupt breweries, the names of which they retained. This explains why certain potteries, somewhat unusually, were called The Three Bells, The Rose, The Peacock and The Greek.

The time was ripe for the production of European porcelain, for the eruption of civil war in China led gradually to a marked decline in exports. Profiting from coincidence, the Dutch potters of the second quarter of the century successfully imitated Chinese porcelain. Delft faience, using tin-glazed enamels, was very delicate and the imitations were of such high quality that they proudly entitled themselves 'makers of porcelain'. In any case, their production was increasingly in demand, known and even exported abroad.

Apart from services and dishes, the faience factories of Delft turned out a wide variety of articles including vases of standard shape and the characteristically long, narrow, tapering tulip-vases, wig-holders and modelled animals which testify to the great talent of their makers. Decoration was in monochrome blue and depicted flowers, birds, landscapes; genre scenes and symbolic signs of Chinese porcelain from the Wanli and Kangxi periods. Imitation of polychrome porcelain initially ran into difficulties, because not all the pigments could withstand high firing, but this problem was overcome by the potters of Delft who decided to complete the underglaze blue decoration with enamels and gilding fixed by a second firing at a temperature that these could tolerate. It was this technique that enabled them to produce the magnificent wall tiles with flower vase motifs and the famous gilded Delftware inspired by Japanese Imari porcelain. They also succeeded with *famille verte* and *famille rose* designs. In endeavouring to imitate the *famille noire* and lacquer objects, they created pieces with a black ground, unique to this period.

## FRANCE

In late seventeenth-century France, ceramics were all the fashion. There were several reasons, not least the fact that as a result of the foreign wars which had drained the treasury, Louis XIV was forced to issue edicts in 1699 and 1709 ordering the melting down of precious plate *see footnote*. The king himself set the example by consigning his own silverware to the furnace and deciding to turn his attention to faience. In imitation of the monarch, the nobility rushed in to buy faience services and other well-to-do families followed suit. There was a sudden and unprecedented demand for the products of Rouen, Moustiers, Marseille and Saint-Cloud, and new workshops were established in Strasbourg, Nideviller, Lille, Sinceny, Sceaux, Chantilly, Vincennes, Sèvres and elsewhere.

The term plate is used for solid silver, or sterling.

The faience wares in the style of Louis XIV were simple in form. Bowls, dishes and flower-pot holders were round, oval or straight-lined. Some pieces were influenced by silverware: larger ones, such as urns and tankards, tended to be heavy and architectural. In addition, there were wares from the Far East. They were adopted and faithfully copied, remaining popular even when they were superseded by French styles.

In fact, thanks to the Dutch and English East India Companies, the import of Chinese blue-and-white porcelain was growing steadily in volume. Its popularity persuaded French faience manufacturers to imitate Chinese designs. In addition to the direct influence of the Far East, there was the shining example of Delft. Indeed, certain special applications for patents mention making faience 'in the Dutch manner'. These sources of inspiration were progressively abandoned in the eighteenth century for *chinoiseries*, new decorative motifs created for the French ornamentalists.

Nevers was the first French ceramic centre to introduce 'Chinese decoration' into its production. This theme was adopted by the majority of other manufacturers, starting with Rouen.

## Rouen

Seventeenth-century Rouen faience is most closely associated with the name of the Poterat family. In 1673 Louis Poterat obtained a new thirty-year patent – a precedent in France – for the manufacture of porcelain: '... to make there all sorts of vessels, pots and vases of porcelain similar to those of China and of violet faience, painted in white, blue and other colours, in the form of that from Holland...' He employed craftsmen of Nevers who introduced Dutch–Chinese designs, used very freely with genuinely French motifs and forms. These included the scalloped lambrequin borders for which Rouen became famous.

▨ Painted plate based on a wall plaque of the early eighteenth century, the golden age of Delft faience. These plaques, produced in pairs, hung on either side of a chimney or door.
The female figures are characteristic. Tall and thin, the *mei-jen*, or 'long ladies', transcend frontiers and are recognisable in the production of neighbouring countries. The women's faces are drawn in red, that of the young boy in blue, according to Chinese fashion. The outlines, which are in manganese violet in the originals, have been done in violet and the red outlines in reddish-brown.
Design by D. Alexiev

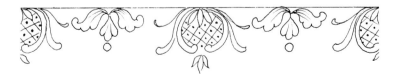

Lambrequin decoration derived from the drapery used for the adornment of canopies (baldaquins) and windows. It was a very skilled and elaborate procedure, justly compared to embroidery. Chinese motifs were clearly important elements in the pattern of lambrequins, which already featured prominently in the decorative range of Delft tableware. The faience manufacturers of Rouen, however, introduced variations to the basic pattern with remarkable skill and originality. Initially in monochrome blue, the lambrequins were enhanced by high-fire colours, plus iron red. Red was notoriously difficult to handle and its outcome doubtful at high temperatures. For this reason, instead of being used flat, it was applied in small touches. Blue was gradually replaced by polychrome decoration.

In the early eighteenth century new manufactories opened in Rouen. The sumptuary laws which ordered the melting down of precious metalware brought commissions for large armorial services in faience. Nevertheless the Oriental influence lingered on. Some designs were borrowed from the *famille verte*, others resorted to the 'horn of plenty' motif, which was widely produced in the middle of the century. These were followed by 'Levantine merchant' pieces, which were less popular because clients preferred porcelain to faience.

## Sinceny

In 1737, Jean-Baptiste de Fayard, lord of Sinceny, decided to set up a pottery. Because he called in makers of faience from Rouen, production from the start was of good quality. Chinese decoration, very much in vogue at the time, helped to assure its success. The designs, based on contemporary Chinese porcelain ware, were adapted for use on pieces that were often typically European. The palette of the *famille verte* or *famille rose* was replaced by the high-fire colour range, dominated by a deep and very rich yellow. The celebrated dish known as the 'Tartar horseman' was made around 1750. It is 55 cm in diameter and shows warriors brandishing their sabres and an oriflamme.

The copy on the facing page was done in two firings: the subject, drawn with sugar mixture in black and reddish-brown, was coloured and fired. A second firing was needed to deepen certain colours. It should be noted that a dark iron red is not absorbed by a deep yellow.

## Saint-Cloud

Research and experiment by French faience manufacturers culminated around 1670 in the discovery of soft-paste porcelain. Louis Poterat appears to have been the first to produce it, but very few soft-paste pieces attributed to Rouen have survived. Independently, Pierre Chicaneau, working at Saint-Cloud, succeeded soon afterwards in

Decoration copied from a Sinceny plate
Design by D. Alexiev

making 'a porcelain almost as perfect as the porcelain of China and the Indies'. These two factories helped to originate many more in France, by reason of craftsmen leaving their employment or moving to other places. Saint-Cloud's production was considerable. Initially it borrowed themes that had brought success to Rouen: radiating designs and lambrequins; but very soon, under the impact of Oriental porcelain, and Japanese in particular, Saint-Cloud began to reproduce virtually the same designs, notably so-called 'Korean' motifs, as those of Chantilly and Meissen.

## Chantilly

Louis-Henri, prince of Condé, an enthusiast of Far Eastern porcelain, particularly that of Japan, was one of the great collectors of his time. Himself a chemist, he was keenly interested in the making of porcelain, and while

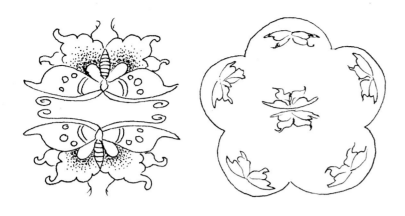

Butterflies. Chantilly reproduced with utmost precision the forms and designs of Japanese models

in exile from political life, in 1726, founded a factory in his château of Chantilly. Ciquaire Cirou, formerly of Saint-Cloud, organised and directed it until his death.

The paste of soft porcelain which he produced at the beginning was a yellowish colour and had to be covered with a white opaque glaze, like faience, to correct this serious flaw. Designs and forms were strongly influenced by Japanese porcelain, especially that produced by Kakiemon. This type of Chantilly decoration is sometimes called 'Korean'.

The famous Condé porcelain collection furnished models which were imitated so perfectly that the prince enjoyed mixing them with the originals. Some models also came from the collection of engravings and drawings that the ornamentalist Fraisse had based on decorative porcelain motifs, on Persian fabrics and on lacquer.

Chantilly, like Saint-Cloud and Meissen, also produced numerous Chinese-style statuettes. Among the best known were the grotesque magots or Poussah, a deformation of Pou-t'ai, the obese god of contentment, shown bearing, or leaning on, his sack of earthly joys.

## Vincennes and Sèvres

The secret of soft-paste porcelain manufacture soon spread to other parts of France. In 1738, the Marquis Orry de Fulvy endeavoured to set up a factory in a disused wing of the château of Vincennes, with two arcanists who had defected from Chantilly, the brothers Gilles and Robert Dubois. Because after three years they had signally failed to achieve the desired results, they were sent home. Research was continued by Francois Gravant who managed, in 1745, to obtain a soft paste which could

be used to make porcelain. This gave rise to the factory of Vincennes, transferred several years later to Sèvres. Louis XV supported and protected the factory and in 1752 awarded it the title of Royal Factory of Porcelain. From this date the royal badge, two crossed L's, became its official mark. The discovery of kaolin deposits at Limousin in 1768–9 promoted the manufacture of hard-paste porcelain. Until 1800, nevertheless, Sèvres continued to produce soft paste ware as well.

The royal factory enjoyed important privileges; and thanks also to competent direction and the collaboration of the finest artists, it went on to gain a worldwide reputation.

The new factory of Vincennes was granted a patent to make porcelain in the 'Chinese manner' and in the 'Saxon manner'. Like so many other manufacturers, it began by imitating Chinese and Kakiemon decoration, as interpreted at Meissen. But Vincennes quickly rid itself of this influence to find its own style and to pursue its own development.

After the death of Louis XIV, there was a transformation of style. Shapes changed and lines became softer and more fluid. Meissonnier, who succeeded Bérain in 1726 as architect and designer of the king's bedchamber and cabinet, created the style of the age: rococo. Water, with its movements, its waves and foam, was the origin of his inspiration. These novel and original ideas were adopted by Duplessis, the royal goldsmith, and his models in the rococo style were faultlessly interpreted in porcelain.

Sèvres boasted a repertory of extraordinary richness and variety. Exotic themes sometimes appeared in its production, but these were no longer motifs imitated from Chinese, Japanese or Saxon porcelain so much as *chinoiseries* of pure fantasy. Several painters from Sèvres specialised in this work, but it did not feature prominently among the factory's major subjects.

*Chinoiseries* were interpreted at Sèvres and subsequently in other factories on rococo pieces. So it is on this type of porcelain that such motifs should be painted.

Gilded chequerwork, stipple, vermiculation and pebblework (*caillouté*) on lapis blue, green and pink backgrounds are among the richest designs created by the artists of Sèvres. Close examination of certain cartouche frames and gildings may reveal elements that are vaguely familiar, namely decorative motifs used by the Chinese

Coffee cups with *chinoiseries*. Design by D. Alexiev
Egg designed by A. Cassagne

Olio pot (1755). Flower arrangements in *chatironné* style: the flowers are outlined like 'India flowers' but have somewhat lost their oriental character. This type of decoration is done in polychrome, in monochrome pink and sometimes in monochrome blue. The bouquet is quite compact but lightened by the graceful flowering sprigs. Notice the harmony of the composition and the thought that has gone into the positioning of the sprigs and stems. These are details that cannot be neglected, for any awkwardness or inaccuracy is immediately evident. Such bouquets make very fresh and pleasant designs and are also easy to do. They are therefore ideal for beginners and highly recommended, too, to all those who have never tackled flowers and are keen to try painting bouquets. The black and white drawing on page 154 shows one of the motifs on the lid. Compose from these elements two slightly different motifs to complete the decoration

The taste for the Far East was no longer so pronounced. This fact and the arrival, in 1748 and 1749, of the two von Löwenfinck brothers, porcelain painters formerly employed at Meissen, gave a new direction to the Strasbourg decorative style. The 'German flowers' made their appearance; these were to develop and be transformed into wonderful floral designs in a purely European style. However, for reasons of profitability, Chinese motifs and bouquets continued to be made as well in flat outlined tints which were less demanding and less costly.

Strasbourg faience immediately made an enormous impact. Its designs were adopted by other manufacturers in eastern France and then crossed the frontier. Thanks to its high artistic quality, it was immensely popular in the rest of Europe, where it was widely sold and imitated.

The Strasbourg representation of a Chinaman does not derive from models of the Far East but from the exotic paintings of Boucher and Pillement. He is a solitary, tranquil individual, a bit on the plump side, busy fishing, chasing butterflies, blowing soap bubbles or peacefully smoking.

When several figures are represented, as often on large dishes, they are not all so easy-going and are often shown fighting. All these activities take place on grassy slopes or among brown and yellow rocks. In 1766 Joseph Hannong was authorised to make porcelain and produced Chinese designs similar to those that had been done on faience.

# GERMANY
## Meissen

The Elector Frederick Augustus I of Saxony, crowned king of Poland as Augustus II the Strong, presided over a court famous for its patronage of art and its love of pomp and luxury, rivalling that of the Sun King himself. Passionately fond of Far Eastern porcelain, Frederick set aside millions from his privy purse to enlarge his collection, and his agents were sent far and wide to purchase Chinese and Japanese porcelain wherever it was available. Naturally he was extremely interested in the work being done throughout Europe to discover the secret of porcelain manufacture.

The celebrated scholar Walter von Tschirnhaus and the alchemist Johann Friedrich Böttger were in the elector's employ and investigated the behaviour of all kinds of materials (metals, rocks and earths) when subjected to fire. At first they managed to turn out a variety of red stoneware, similar to that already manufactured at Delft around 1680. Fine and hard, it could be cut, engraved or polished on the wheel, enabling motifs to be made in relief. It quickly became popular. Decorated with gold, with varnish or with black lacquer applied cold, these pieces were European in form with designs inspired by Chinese art.

In the course of these efforts to produce white porcelain, Tschirnhaus died. Next year, 1709, the experiments met with success. Böttger fired a white clay which turned out to be kaolin. He attempted to mix it with alabaster, then with feldspar, and eventually found the right proportions to produce a new material, similar to Chinese porcelain, which he treated with a suitable glaze. This was the first example in Europe of hard-paste porcelain. On 23 January 1710, a highly satisfied Frederick Augustus officially announced the news of the important discovery. The town of Dresden, under the elector's rule, was one of the great art centres of Europe. Without delay, a factory was set up in the castle of Meissen; hence the reason why the two names were applied to its products.

Following this momentous breakthrough, the next step was to imitate the underglaze blue decoration of Chinese porcelain and Delft faience. One thousand écus were promised as a reward to anyone who discovered the secret. Despite all research and experiment, it was not until after the death of Böttger that a positive result, though not yet wholly satisfactory, was obtained. There had been many problems to overcome. The first colours were dull and heavy, and Böttger himself rarely used them. Furthermore, until 1720, there was no recognised painter at the factory.

During this difficult period, the best designs were done outside the factory. Böttger sent white porcelain wares to Augsburg to be mounted in gold and silver. The

■ Motifs derived from the decorative repertory of the Du Paquier period, still employed in the factory of Vienna. The India flowers are used for decorating services

goldsmiths of the town, who had a deserved reputation, went even further by painting the pieces in gold and silver. The designs were then chased and the motifs accentuated by the delicate interplay of light and shade. The subjects were Chinese, accompanied by baroque ornaments such as lambrequins and latticework.

Many of these *chinoiseries*, as well as later polychrome decorations, were done by the so-called Hausmaler, designers working at home, to whom the factories sent their white porcelain. Painting as a cottage industry was very common at Meissen and Vienna, and local designers included some remarkable painters.

Nevertheless, until the arrival of Johann Gregorius Höroldt at Meissen in 1720, painted decoration on porcelain remained very mediocre, for the colours were muddy and lacked sparkle. Höroldt came from the Vienna factory and within a few years, thanks to his experience and talent, he put together a palette of exceptionally luminous, brilliant colours. Among the characteristic light colours of Meissen porcelain in its first period were sky-blue, glaucous, soft green, rust, lemon yellow, purple and brown.

It was then that the beautiful *à la chinoise* designs appeared. Like the prince of Condé, Frederick Augustus I supplied the Meissen painters with models from his collection. Many of the Japanese motifs in the Kakiemon style were fine, precise copies of these models, done on genuine porcelain, and almost indistinguishable from the originals. There were designs, too, from the repertories of the Saint-Cloud and Chantilly factories, as for example the hedge motif. But Höroldt competed with these designs by introducing his own *chinoiseries*. In 1726, in fact, he published a collection of engravings in which he represented Chinese figures of pure fantasy in a very special and recognisable style. His characters, thin, long-limbed and dressed in rich costumes, are shown smoking, drinking tea, fishing, chatting and occupying themselves in all manner of ways against a decorative background of exotic trees, gigantic flowers and strange birds. This assemblage of Chinese types gradually came to feature not only in the designs of Meissen but also in those of other factories which rapidly sprang up in Germany. Each of the painters who specialised in this genre succeeded in bringing to it his individual touch, contributing to the success of *chinoiseries*.

After 1740, however, the fashion for everything Chinese waned and Meissen was subjected to the stronger influence of European products, particularly that of French porcelain. Meissen was determined to guard its secret of porcelain manufacture and adopted strict measures of security. Even so, the secret leaked out and quickly spread across Europe. This was hardly surprising since for years ceramists everywhere had been following their own lines of research. The number of manufactories established elsewhere in no way detracted from the importance of Meissen in developing the art of porcelain, and indeed its pioneering influence was pervasive.

In the ensuing centuries the fortunes of Meissen fluctuated in response to historical events, and today it remains one of the world's most prestigious manu-facturers.

Shortly after the Meissen enterprise, a factory in Vienna succeeded in turning out an almost identical type of hard-paste porcelain. Two former Meissen employees arrived there and not only assisted Claude Innocent du Paquier in founding a factory in 1718 but also procured the necessary kaolin from Saxony.

The production of the Du Paquier period (1718–44) was marked by the baroque style, the influence of Daniel Marot and Jean Bérain, and also the great Austrian architects. Decoration was based essentially on the Oriental repertory, but the flower bouquets soon made their appearance, introducing the European theme.

*Chinoiserie en vert* and *chinoiserie* were the names of this decoration from the Vienna factory. They were employed for table services, the motif set in the centre of the plates occupying not more than half of the bowl. The rim is adorned with a broad band (5 mm), accentuated by a very narrow fillet.

## ENGLAND

The influence of Delft was felt in all neighbouring countries. The English faience manufacturers copied or imitated Delft blue-and-white so skilfully that their production came to be known as Delftware. The motifs illustrated in black and white on the facing page are taken or adapted from English underglaze blue pieces. Blue-and-white ware of this type was widely produced in the eighteenth century in Liverpool, Lowestoft and Caughley. Some of these designs were also interpreted in polychrome. The first motif, 'The Peony', was used at Plymouth and later, in 1775–80, was produced in colour by printing based on the original version from Worcester.

Porcelain appeared in England around 1740. Conditions here were very different from those on the continent. English manufactories were private enterprises and benefited neither from the protection nor financial assistance of kings or noble patrons, as was the case almost everywhere in Europe, particularly France, Germany and Italy. Thus English manufacturers faced

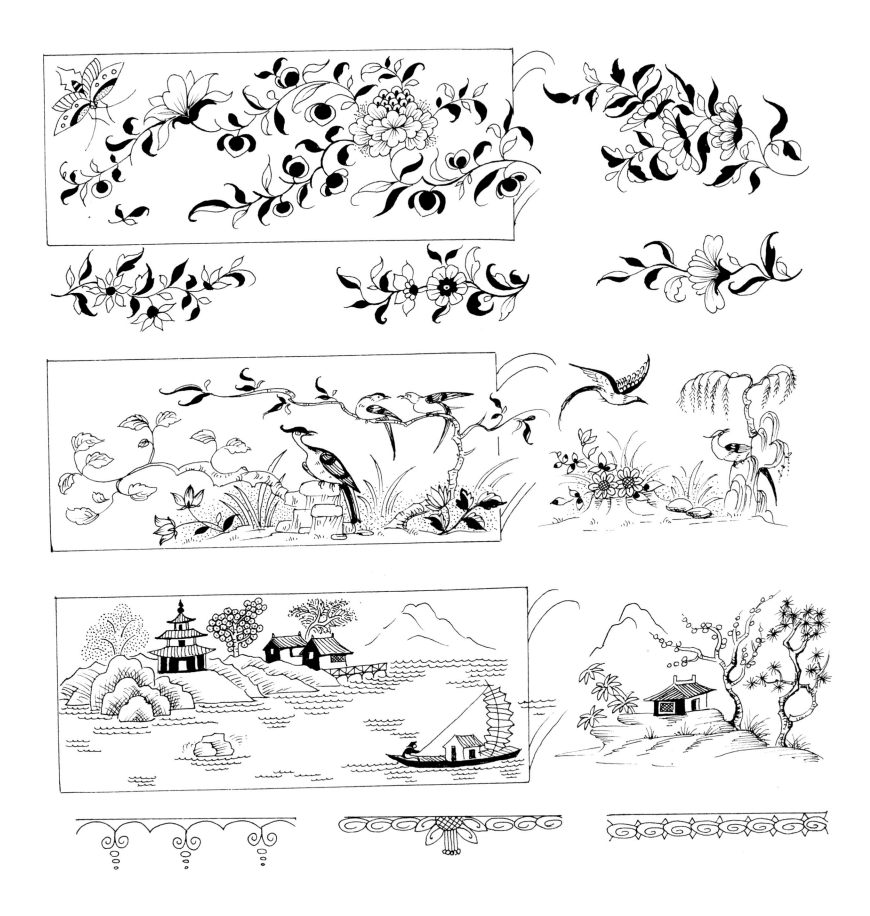

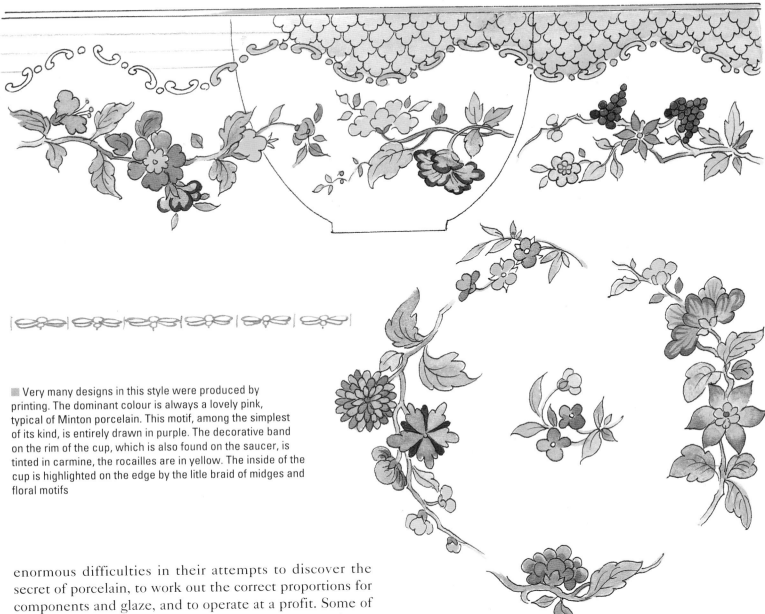

Very many designs in this style were produced by printing. The dominant colour is always a lovely pink, typical of Minton porcelain. This motif, among the simplest of its kind, is entirely drawn in purple. The decorative band on the rim of the cup, which is also found on the saucer, is tinted in carmine, the rocailles are in yellow. The inside of the cup is highlighted on the edge by the little braid of midges and floral motifs

enormous difficulties in their attempts to discover the secret of porcelain, to work out the correct proportions for components and glaze, and to operate at a profit. Some of them failed to sustain the economic effort for more than a year or two. Indeed, there were so many setbacks that of the fifteen factories founded in England up to 1780, only two survived into the nineteenth century.

Taking into account these circumstances, very few of the English factories had the advantage of an initial production comparable to that enjoyed by their continental counterparts. Some of them stuck to the simpler forms and decorative style of faience, so that their products remained accessible to a wide public. Others, such as Chelsea, Derby and Worcester, produced fine porcelain that initially followed the influence of Meissen and later that of Sèvres.

The taste for tea spread through Europe some 200 years ago. Originally the plant grew only in China and not until much later was it cultivated elsewhere. Practised by the Chinese since ancient times and associated with many legends, tea drinking became a ceremony and even an art during the T'ang period. In China it remained an occasion for pleasure and relaxation, whereas in Japan,

Teapot. The model is taken from a piece produced at Worcester between 1765 and 1775. Note the Kakiemon motifs in the brocaded style Design by A. Cassagne

where it was introduced by the Zen sect, it was governed by very strict rules of protocol.

The drinking of tea and its celebration contributed to the development of ceramics in the Orient and later in the West with the creation of receptacles and of specific forms.

As everywhere, there was a call in England for Chinese and Japanese designs. English ceramic products displayed the Kakiemon motifs dear to Meissen and certain French factories, such as the hedge, exotic birds, flowers and trees of the Orient. Under the influence of French artists, *chinoiseries*, particularly those in gold on coloured grounds, as created by Sèvres, made an appearance.

After initial hardships, the English porcelain industry grew by leaps and bounds, and production was extremely prolific and varied. As on the continent in the nineteenth century, there was a marked revival of exoticism and a new wave of Chinese-style and Imari motifs.

## ITALY

Europe, as we have seen, was fascinated by Chinese porcelain and attempts to discover the secrets of the new

substance and to imitate it were pursued everywhere. The first experiments were made in Florence under the patronage of Francesco de' Medici. They culminated in a satisfactory result: a soft ivory- or grey-coloured paste. Very few of these products remain. The designs are monochrome, in blue (cobalt oxide) or brown (manganese oxide) under a lead glaze. The motifs are of Oriental, Ottoman or Persian inspiration, or based on current fashion, such as grotesques or armorial compositions. The activity of the Florentine factory was of short duration, from 1575 to 1611.

The first hard-paste porcelain to be made in Italy was at the Vezzi factory of Venice in 1720. It was made of kaolin from Auë, which supplied Meissen. The production was of very beautiful quality but the factory had to close some years later because of financial problems.

▒ Motif taken from a dish from Ginori
Design by M. Lombardo

## JAPANISM

In the nineteenth century there was a revival of rococo. Forms and designs were usually heavy and overloaded. There were practically no new trends. Broadly speaking, European porcelain went through a rather depressed period.

Towards 1870 a reaction set in against this lack of creative endeavour. Unconnected with *chinoiseries*, the Japanese representation of flowers and animals began to assume prime importance in Europe. European painters and illustrators greatly admired the precision and strength of designs reduced to their essential elements and, above all, there was the discovery of nature as a source of inexhaustible variety. Japanese art was a revelation and there were many who preached the overriding virtues of Japanese forms of decoration.

Japan, like China beforehand, published a large number of treatises on painting. These images were widely diffused and contributed to the development of a new artistic vision.

International expositions and fairs in Europe and America did much to spread and popularise Japanese art. Ancient Japanese works of art were regularly exhibited. Moreover, collectors such as Jules Jacquemard and Emile Guimet also exhibited Japanese masterpieces. Siegfried (Samuel) Bing, a businessman, was a great lover of the Oriental arts. He published a magazine, *Artistic Japan*, in which were reproduced many prints by Hokusai and Uyamaro. Artists were overwhelmed by such discoveries and the new trend of Japanism followed in their wake.

Japan exercised an influence not only on painting but also on the decorative arts. The engraver Félix Bracquemond adopted Japanese art themes and concepts, introducing the trend to the field of ceramics. His plates 'in the Japanese style' inspired the faience dinner service made

Research continued in the faience works and new factories such as those of Nove de Bassano, Cozzi, etc. and in the course of the eighteenth century true porcelain was produced. Motifs of Chinese and Japanese inspiration were followed in Italy by the fashion for *chinoiserie*, but this was not much pursued.

In 1737 the Marquis Carlo Ginori founded a factory at Doccia, near Florence. The experimental work he pursued was not very conclusive. On a visit to Vienna, however, he engaged the painter Carl Anreiter and Giorgio delle Torri, kiln worker and modeller for Du Paquier. Production commenced soon afterwards and from 1745 Ginori porcelain was sold throughout Europe. The factory remained family property until 1876. It then joined with the Milanese firm of Richard and the products of the Richard-Ginori factory still enjoy great prestige to this day.

■ Models produced by Gien in underglaze blue, here interpreted in polychrome. The bamboo that adorns the edge is not the only element of the Far East. The floral subject, the naturalist treatment and the layout are inspired by Japanese motifs
Design by T. de Ternoy

by Eugène Rousseau, and opened the way to new ideas. The Japanese designer always started with an expressive, precise outline which contained all the characteristic details. This gave the design great clarity. The method allowed him, also, to arrange the pattern in a very decorative manner, according to individual inspiration. This type of representation was adopted in Europe in the area of glass, particularly of the ornamental vase. Emile Gallé, as well as the Daum brothers, were greatly inspired by it and sometimes copied certain pictures of Japanese botanic painters.

Stylisation born of attentive observation and sobriety of composition were the characteristics of the Art Nouveau style. It was to triumph at the Paris Universal Exposition of 1900 and reached its peak in the years leading up to the First World War. Interest in this very recognisable style was revived during the inter-war period.

It is self-evident that art knows no frontiers. Europe, as we have seen, was at various times under the total sway of the Orient, and the influence of the latter was strongly felt in many fields. In the eighteenth century the cult of exoticism infiltrated both literature and music. In the nineteenth century it was the culture of Japan that gave fresh impetus to many European painters and craftsmen. Although, in the overall context, the impact of the Far East was not paramount, the artistic treasures produced by these civilisations continue to be a source of boundless inspiration.

▨ Vase with young vine inspired by a glass vase produced by the Technical School of Steinschönau. In the 1900s style, the parts based on nature are extremely stylised; they can be adapted successfully for many decorative forms
Design by D. Alexiev

LARGE ENAMELED DISHES

63, 64. (facing page) Large enameled Nabeshima dish, peony, rock and flowerpot design.
D. 30.9 cm. Kurita Art Museum.

65, 66. Large enameled Nabeshima dish, treasures design. D. 30.3 cm. Okayama Art
Museum.

67. Large enameled Nabeshima dish, peach design. D. 31.2 cm. Kyūori Atami Art Museum.

68. Large enameled Nabeshima dish, mandarin orange design. Kyūori Atami
Art Museum.

# Technical Index

## BANDS

The most simple way of finishing a piece is to accentuate its rim with a band of varying width either in colour or in gold. There may be several bands on the same piece, for they are used to separate or emphasise the different parts of the object or the design. Learning how to make bands (also called fillets) is an essential part of porcelain decoration.

**Bands for round objects** Such bands are made with a tournette or banding wheel. This is a precision instrument composed of a circular steel turntable rotating on its axis. The turntable has a short axis while that of the stand-mounted turntable is long, making it possible to fix the turntable at different heights.

**Bands for tall objects** To do these, the turntable must be raised and lowered. The band should be placed at the right height, i.e. within reach of the brush when the hand rests on the piece.

**Bands for plates** According to their position, it is convenient to be able to alter the height of the turntable. Thus for bands inside a plate, fix the platter beneath the level of the table so that, when holding the brush vertically, its point touches the surface. For bands on the rim of the plate, fix the turntable at the same height as the table and hold the brush horizontally, so as to utilise the full length of the tuft.

▧ Almost completed Nabeshima plate
Design by J. Fournier

The first condition for making a band successfully is to centre the object perfectly on the wheel. The concentric grooves marked on the turntable help to position it. If, however, the piece covers the whole turntable, as would be the case with a large dish, proceed as follows: start the wheel, slide the fingertip over the rim of the dish while keeping the hand still, leaning on the table. Correct its position as necessary by pushing gently as it moves. When the revolving rim is no longer fluctuating against your finger (which is acting as a static benchmark) this indicates the right position. Since plates are not always perfect, slight stops and starts may be inevitable.

The second condition is to keep the position stable. The hand should exert steady pressure on the brush. This ensures that the band will be uniformly thick and regular. To acquire the necessary confidence, keep the elbow and hand resting on the table.

To do the band, place the tip or tuft, depending on the case, of the loaded brush on the correct spot and with the other hand push the turntable in an anti-clockwise direction. If left-handed, turn it from right to left. When the table has made a complete circuit, the end of the band should meet the beginning. Its thickness must be even.

Special brushes are essential, which are long, pointed or chamfered. Place the chamfered side towards the surface of the piece. To find it, merely flatten the loaded brush against the palette.

Bands can be made in colour or with precious metals. Success and quality depend likewise on the preparation of the colours or the brilliance of the gold. Here are a few guidelines:

The colour should contain less fatty substance and enough thin oil to be sufficiently fluid. The band must emerge from behind the brush cleanly and without a break, making a circuit in one go. It should quickly become matt and dry. If it 'runs' or remains shiny, wipe out and correct the preparation by adding powder colour. Sugar mixture colours can also be added.

Sometimes the colour is paler near the end of the band; to unify the tone make a half circuit or a complete circuit without lifting the brush and without adding more colour.

Thickness is fatal: the bands flake. Before doing a new band, clean off thoroughly the one that has flaked.

Precious metals (gold, platinum) are liquid, therefore easier to use. Before commencing, see that the product is homogeneous. Like colour, gold can lose its depth near the end of the band. Sometimes this is difficult to notice. If in the slightest doubt, reload the brush and go over the part again. If the gold is not consistent enough, it fades after firing.

To avoid the trouble of going over a band again, always use a brush that is of the same thickness as the band to be painted, and is thick enough to hold sufficient colour to complete the band. Cheap porcelain tends to be flawed, which sometimes mars the quality of the bands. For example:

a) For a tall object (lamp, vase) that leans or is irregular: after centralising, do the band by supporting the piece. Thus, by resting a fimger lightly on the surface, it is possible to follow the movement of the porcelain, to regulate it and cope with deviations of the brush.
b) A plate that is not perfectly flat will have an irregular band: thin or thick as the wing moves up or down. To remedy this fault, before starting work, mark out the position of the band around the rim with a pencil. Do not overrun this guide mark. When doing the band, watch carefully and reduce or increase brush pressure as necessary.

Bands for variously shaped objects must be done by hand. Trace in pencil the guide line and, firmly supporting the turntable and the piece, draw the band. To avoid several attempts, use a band brush or any brush that suits the purpose.

Transparent adhesive tape can be used to make the job easier. Stick it along the whole length of the line defining the band, so as to protect the white part. The operation requires precision and patience.

**Circular bands in the centre of variously shaped objects** It is impossible to centralise on the turntable an object that is not round. In this case, a compass is needed to frame the central motif with a circular band.

Draw diagonals: the point where they meet is the centre of the piece. Stick several layers of transparent adhesive tape over it to find the exact place and to fix the compass properly. Load the drawing pen with colour and sketch the necessary number of circles.

If a banding wheel is unavailable, the compass can be used for the inside of plates. Find and mark in pencil the

diameter with a ruler: it passes through the most distant opposite points. Draw a second diameter. The point where the two intersect is the centre of the plate. Then proceed as explained above. In order to work conveniently with a compass, the colour must be sufficiently liquid, so use a preparation that contains little fatty matter or that used for drawing with a sugar mixture. Whether or not bands are enjoyable to do, there is no going back. Learning comes with late application and patience, and there is the satisfaction of greater and greater success.

## COLOURS

The designs painted on the glaze of porcelain or the enamel of faience are 'third or low-fire' designs. They withstand relatively low firing at 800°–850°C. This temperature is tolerated by a large number of oxides and permits a very rich palette of colours.

Colours are composed of a colouring element (metallic oxide) and a fusible element (flux), ground into extremely fine powders and then mixed perfectly.

When fired, the flux fuses with the glaze or enamel and definitively fixes the oxide. Lead fluxes combine best with the glaze, making the colours brilliant and oily. The lead content – an element that entails some danger – tends to be diminished or almost eliminated in most colours. This is one reason for the difference to be noted when comparing results with brightly coloured pieces made in the past.

Colours, whether with or without lead, give good results only if they are correctly employed. There are various rules that have to be observed:

- Each colour should be used in the depth indicated on the colour chart at time of purchase. For example, a bright, deep blue should not be used to paint a forget-me-not, a pale blue sky or to do a light tint. It would result in a rough, matt and, in most cases, satiny surface.
- All colours should be applied quite thickly to give the best results.
- A layer of colour that is too thick will flake or fire badly.
- A layer of colour that is too thin will remain matt and is not solid; when used it dilutes and fades away.
- It is important to know the peculiarities of certain colours.

Characteristics to bear in mind. The gold family groups together all colours that contain varying quantities of purple, which is made with gold. They have the following properties:

allergy to turpentine, use the pure oil, available from a specialised shop for painting materials.

- Oil such as eugenol (oil of cloves) or lavender will keep preparations fluid, either for painting or cleaning.
- Ready-made products for drawing have certain advantages. Some can be fired before painting, provided their fluidity is stable. Others can be coloured as soon as they are dry but need to be strengthened to 'hold' well: add a very little sugar.
- Resist is used to protect one or two of the colour surfaces, generally applied by tinting. It can be applied to the following:
  a) a surface that needs to be kept white in the middle of a coloured ground;
  b) around a shape that is to be tinted, in the middle of a white ground.
  For example, before tinting a large elephant grey, surround the design with a good centimetre of varnish. In this way the outlines will be sharp and not need cleaning.
  Do not tint so long as the resist sticks to the fingers.
  Detach the film before the tint is completely dry.
  Remove and clean, leaving no trace of resist.
- Methylated spirit is used to degrease pieces and clean traces of painting. It is advisable to use a good pointed brush reserved exclusively for methylated spirit

## PEN DRAWING

Outlines and details of a motif done in colour are often drawn with a pen. The colour must therefore be fluid enough for drawing long lines and for following the design easily.

**Types of pen** The two simplest and most frequently used forms of drawing are the following:

1 Oil-based pen. Make a compact mixture with colour and a little fat oil, add a couple of drops of eugenol. Use turpentine to give the necessary fluidity for writing. Do a test: a thick and bright line or a drop of colour at the tip of the pen indicate too much 'fat'. It is difficult to draw with a fat colour and furthermore the result is bad. Add a little powder to correct the mixture. A thin, continuous line which dries quickly shows that the colour is right. Maintain this consistency. Rework the colour from time to time to soften it; if insufficient, add a little turpentine.
This drawing, very well dried, may be coloured provided care is taken: turpentine and oils (lavender, etc.) dissolve it. For quality work it is best to fix the motif by firing prior to painting.

2 Sugar-based pen. Mix the colour with about one-sixth as much icing sugar and water. Use the spatula to melt the sugar. Do a test: draw, let it dry for five minutes and pass the finger over it. The lines should resist gentle rubbing. If they are wiped out, add a very little sugar and try again. Too much sugar makes the work difficult and moreover the drawing that results may have points that jut out or even flake when fired.
The 'sugar' drawing dries rapidly and can be fired without a previous firing. Another important advantage is that these colours last indefinitely. Simply add a little water and they are ready for use. However, when the lines show signs of becoming pale, make a fresh colour to maintain the clarity of the drawing.

**Colour of the drawing** The majority of motifs suggested in this book, based on or inspired by ancient pieces, are *chatironnés*. The drawing is often done in black or manganese violet. This ranges in depth from brown-black to light aubergine. For this type of drawing there are two choices:

a) Black is suitable both for monochrome and polychrome subjects and is the form of drawing most often employed. Like all colours, black exists in various shades and for drawings it is best to use the least dark. It is possible to make one's own 'drawing black' by mixing:
  • three parts black and one part carmine;
  • dark green and purple, which produces a blackish green.
b) If black is to be avoided, use violet or a dark reddish-brown.

These colours serve to outline and give detail to subjects, without taking into account the different tints that may be used later. Often the parts of the motif are drawn with different colours. For example, branches and leaves are drawn in black or brown; the flowers are *chatironnés*, with tints corresponding to the colour of each motif.

- For parts painted in all shades of pale pink to purple, choose for the drawing tints ranging from light grey to deep carmine (reinforced with purple). Avoid pure purples, which produce drawings that are too dark. In certain motifs from the Far East the pink flowers are surrounded by red; to do these choose a medium iron red and do not let the areas touch.
- To draw the red parts, use the colour which will serve for painting even if it is a light one: the colour in the

■ Plates with prunus decoration, done by tinting in three firings:
1 Position the flowers, buds and branches. Cover with resist glaze. Tint. Remove the glaze. Fire.
2 Cover with resist glaze the flowers and buds that are to be left white. Tint with a very thin layer of the colour used for the first tinting. Fire.
3 Do the flower pistils in gold. Fire.
The fillets do not obtrude: the edge of the tinted area is neat and regular, the wing adequately decorated and, moreover, this is a contemporary interpretation
Design by D. Alexiev

drawings is always deeper. Never make outlines in yellow or grey: they absorb the red when fired and the outlines take on a faded, blurred tint.

- In certain classical motifs, the outlines of yellow parts are in brown, black or purple. If less emphatic lines are required, use grey, light green or brownish-yellow.

Warning: in the model the parts of the design coloured yellow are outlined and detailed in red. Pale yellows absorb red, a very fragile colour when it is light. So choose a dark red, fix the drawing by firing and to colour the subject take a medium or dark yellow. Do not use selenium-based reds. (See **Colours – Reds**).

- Draw the green parts in black, with one of the outline colours or with brown. If green is used, it should not be garish and, for the necessary contrast, it is best to choose one that is dark or neutral.
- Coloured parts in blue. Look at the model and do the outline in the same colour or choose for the drawing a fairly dark tone, depending on the colour to be used for painting.
- Gold can also be used for drawing and detailing subjects painted in colour. Use the pen or a fine brush, but before beginning this work for the first time, consult sections on **Gold** and **Firing**.
- Metallic colours can be used for drawing but only as a finish, after firing the colours.

## PREPARATION OF COLOURS

Paints are sold in the form of powders and have to be used in conjunction with binding materials such as fat oil or an oil-based medium. The method of preparation changes according to the product chosen. In the following instructions for mixtures, it is impossible to indicate exact proportions, and personal experiment will be necessary.

1 Colour and fat oil: these make a fairly thick, soft and glossy mixture, but not one that runs. This product can even be kept for more than a fortnight in the covered pots sold for this purpose. Proceed as follows:
a) Dilute the colour with turpentine (white spirit) and bring it to the consistency needed for the work in hand.
b) Apply the colour with a brush slightly moistened with an essential oil (eugenol, lavender, etc.).
After loading the brush – though not to excess – spread the colour evenly. Its surface should rapidly become matt. Brilliance indicates that the colour is too fat (rectify by adding powder) or that it has been applied too thickly (thin the layer).

2 Colour, turpentine and fat oil: moisten the colour with the turpentine to obtain a soft paste. Add a very little fat oil; the colour will become fluid. This preparation, which spreads easily, dries quickly and the proper consistency has to be maintained by adding turpentine and also, if need be, more fat oil. The colour eventually becomes greasy and, in order to do the job easily and well, it is best to prepare small quantities and then to make more.

3 Mediums for painting are products designed to facilitate work and avoid errors caused by preparations that are too fatty. The characteristics change from one product to another and so does the manner of preparing the colour. Proceed as follows:
a) Mix colour and medium to give immediate fluidity suitable for the work in hand. When the product dries, add more thinner.
b) Mix colour and medium to obtain a pasty consistency, and provide the necessary fluidity by adding turpentine. It is identical to the preceding preparation with fat oil but the colours do not keep so long.

The quantity of binder used to prepare a colour also depends on the use to be made of it. For filling in, a dry (not too fatty) and liquid colour is best, while for modelling it should be balanced and supple. For tinting large pieces it is advisable to use a slightly fatty colour so as to have time to obtain a perfectly uniform surface, and for delicate retouching it will need to be adjusted so that it does not smear when fired. Experience, and even error, are the best guides.

## TINTING

The technique of tinting is designed to obtain coloured grounds and is applied in order to change, either partially or entirely, the colour of an object. Tinting is also employed to give a colour a consistent, uniform appearance, even over a small surface.
Tinting is done with a sable brush or, more commonly, with a more easily manageable silk or synthetic pad.

1 Small surfaces do not require any special colour preparation. To colour and unify a subject (as, for example, fruits, flowers, leaves, faces, etc.), gently pat all over with the brush or pad.
2 Average surfaces (small objects, ornaments, borders, etc.) should be tinted with a normal preparation, as for painting, but slightly more fluid. Distribute the colour with a brush and tint with the pad.
3 Large surfaces require more care and preparation.

- The work table and all materials (tiles, brushes, knives) must be thoroughly cleaned and in good working order. Use a new pad and make sure the turpentine is clear. Avoid wearing woollen clothing that may shed fluff.
- Calculate the amount of colour that will be needed. It is better to have a little too much than not enough. Work procedure, whatever preparation is used, will be along the same lines.

**Preparations with fat oil** The two variations already suggested (see **Preparation of Colours**) can be employed for tinting, but which of the two to use is a matter for personal decision. As a general rule, these mixtures should be more oily so as to allow time for the colour to spread over the whole surface and then to be smoothed with the pad.

When using the first preparation, soften the colour with a few drops of eugenol or lavender oil which help to give and maintain fluidity. Stir the paste vigorously for some time. Add turpentine and mix in thoroughly: the colour should not 'stick' but allow the brush to slide smoothly. Quickly prepare the pad: sprinkle (but do not soak) with turpentine and roll between the palms of the hands. It should just be moist. Take a large flat brush and cover the entire surface as uniformly as possible. Then dab with the pad, initially to rub out the brush marks and then, more carefully, to get rid of the marks left by the pad.

The second preparation, very fluid from the start, should merely contain a little more fat oil.

**Preparations with a medium** Make up the colour according to the quality of the medium (see **Preparation of Colours**), adding neither eugenol nor lavender oil. It is not necessary to dampen the pad.

Flux, added to preparations, makes the colours more brilliant.

**Useful advice:**

- Allow the resist, if being used, to dry before proceeding to tint.
- Wipe the tile and table clean of all traces of dust from the colours.
- Test the colour before applying it to the whole surface.
  a) If the tinting mixture looks like the skin of an orange, it is too fat, lacks turpentine, or combines both faults.
  b) If the mixture looks dry or strips off, it is not fat enough. In both cases, rectify the mixture so as not to spoil the piece. While engaged in tinting, take care to:
- concentrate hard and work quickly.

The pinks of Iznik: black drawing

- correct faults before the colour dries. Even so, it is not easy to do this without leaving marks. If the tinted surface is not to be covered by a design, it is best to begin again. Virtually all accidents occur at the cleaning stage.

a) Do not wait until the tint is dry to remove hairs, dust, etc. Use a pair of fine tweezers or a wax crayon, pressing the tip over the affected spot. Remove immediately so as not to tear away and tint lightly if necessary.

b) Wait until the tint has dried slightly before removing specks of resist. Use a needle or, better still, tweezers. Above all, do not forget the specks trapped beneath the tint: resist leaves marks after firing.

c) Clean the piece carefully so that no trace of glaze or colour remains. If the edges are to be kept white, clean only when the tint is dry. This is to avoid creating blobs of colour which make marks and flake.

### TRANSFERRING

This is a method of making several or unlimited numbers of faithful copies of a drawing, using a variety of techniques:

### With tracing paper and wax crayon

1 Place the tracing paper over the model to be reproduced and copy the outlines and important details with a coloured crayon.

2 Turn the sheet upside down and go over the drawing seen in transparency, with a wax crayon for porcelain.

3 Fix the transfer to the piece with adhesive tape. Go over the tracing with an ordinary black pencil. The colour tracing which remains visible indicates that this spot has not been gone over with the black pencil.

4 It is possible from the start to copy the motif with a porcelain crayon and to use the transfer, but the image is inverted and this is often annoying when it comes to painting. To avoid this, there are alternative methods.

### With tracing and carbon paper

1 Copy the model on tracing paper with an ordinary black pencil (H). Fix the transfer to the chosen place, slipping the carbon paper between the piece and the transfer.

2 Before beginning the transfer, make sure to exert the correct pressure: make a mark in the corner and lift the sheets to see how clearly it has come out. The tracing, but nothing more, should be visible.

3 Go over the whole tracing methodically with a fine point which leaves no marks (used biro tip, tip of boxwood stick etc.). This preserves the precision of the transfer which can be used indefinitely.

Note: a tracing that is too heavy may spoil the rest of the work.

It is advisable to use graphite or ordinary black carbon paper. Blue carbon should be avoided: used as a guide mark for gold work, it almost always leaves marks after firing.

### Pouncing

1 Copy the motif on tracing paper. Prick the entire tracing with a very fine needle: the holes should be tiny and quite close together.

2 Fix the prepared pouncing to the chosen spot. Go over it with a pounce (roller made with a band of closely woven material or a small pad of silk) lightly soaked in charcoal powder: the motif will be transcribed in dots on to the piece.

Pouncing does not deteriorate with use and is employed in workshops to obtain an exact and permanent copy of a model. Its origin is unknown but it undoubtedly goes back to early times.

# *Glossary*

ALBARELLO Cylindrically shaped druggists' jar. The Italian term may be a rendering of the Persian word for a spice jar, *el barani*.

BISCUIT Unglazed porcelain with a matt surface. The term has two possible meanings but only the second one given below is strictly correct:
a) Biscuit or bisque are names given to porcelain that has undergone a first firing of 1000°C in order to dehydrate it before glazing. However, the Italian word *biscotto* is literally 'fired twice' and applied only to porcelain.
b) Porcelain definitively fired at 1400°C, thus vitrified but not glazed. This type of porcelain, produced in 1750 at Vincennes, was mass produced at Sèvres and was subsequently adopted in other large factories in the eighteenth century.

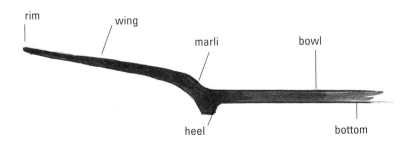

Sections of a plate.

BISQUE Any earthenware object which has undergone an initial half-firing. It is hard and porous, ready to be glazed.

BONE CHINA Semi-hard English porcelain, so called because of the bone ash used in its composition (about 40 per cent). Since it did not display the drawbacks of French soft porcelain, it continued to be made and was subsequently adopted in other countries such as Sweden and Germany.

BURNISH To polish gold or platinum which is dull or matt after firing porcelain.

CAILLOUTE Decorative motif utilised at Sèvres, consisting of tiny oval crescents in gold, usually on a dark blue ground.

CAMAIEU Painted monochrome decoration in different shades of the chosen colour.

CASSIUS PURPLE Colour obtained from gold chloride, discovered in the seventeenth century by Andréas Cassius, a chemist from Leyden in Holland.

CELADON Chinese ceramic dating from the Han period. Its greenish colour came from the iron oxide present in the clay. From the Song dynasty onwards, it denoted stoneware with this translucent glaze.

CERAMIC From the Greek word for baked clay, *keramos*. It was adopted in the eighteenth century as a generic term for any earthenware object which, when subjected to a temperature above 600°C, underwent a complete and definitive physical and chemical transformation. Thus it comprises products such as terracotta, faience, stoneware and porcelain. Their characteristic differences determine to which of two major categories they belong: porous ceramics (pottery and faience) and hard, impermeable, vitrified paste ceramics (stoneware and porcelain).

CHATIRON A stroke made generally in black or manganese and used for drawing motifs on faience or porcelain, e.g. *fleurs chatironnées*. Painted flowers without contour lines are known as *fleurs fines*.

CLAY Sedimentary earthy rock formed mainly by the decomposition of silicates of aluminium under the action of water and carbonic acid. When soaked with water it becomes malleable. The presence of a mineral substance (iron oxide, magnesium, etc.) gives clay its colour.

COUVERTE A hard coating which covers porcelain. Applied to the biscuit (once-fired clayware), it fires and vitrifies at 1400°C at the same time as the porcelain body.

CUERDA SECA (dry cord) Spanish term to describe a decorative technique introduced by the Arabs. Used in making tiles, it consisted of outlining the motifs with a mixture of black or manganese and fat to prevent the colours mingling in the course of firing. The black stroke gave precision to the design and emphasised, by contrast, the luminosity of the colours.

DAIMYO Title given to the feudal princes of ancient Japan.

ENGOBE Technique which entails masking the colour of the paste but which is also used for decoration. Engobe is a mixture of very pure liquid clay, quartz and water, used for covering terracotta. White or slightly tinted, it can be given different tones of yellow, orange or red. It is possible to colour it with manganese dioxide (brown, black) and cobalt oxide (blue).
Decoration is done by brush with thinned engobe. It can be applied directly on to the paste or on to an engobed surface. Engobing is done on unfired clay pieces.
This technique was very widespread prior to the discovery of tin glazes.

FAIENCE Porous paste ceramic entirely covered with opaque tin glaze which renders it impermeable. Originating in the Middle East (Assyrian decorated wall facings), this technique was not utilised by the Romans but developed in Persia. It was introduced to Europe by the Arabs who settled in Spain. The famous Hispano-Moresque faience exported in the fourteenth century to Italy came from Manises, Malaga and Majorca: it was known as maiolica. Production in Italy began in the fifteenth century in several towns, including Faenza, hence the new name.
The word 'faience' is a generic term. There is a distinction between *grand feu* (high-fire) and *petit feu* (low-fire) faience, depending upon the decorative technique emplyed. Moreover, from the seventeenth century, the faience known as Delftware, originating in England, was composed of a fine white clay covered simply with a transparent lead glaze.

FELDSPAR Natural aluminosilicates of potassium, sodium and calcium. It is a component of the paste and glaze of porcelain.

FRIT Vitreous substance obtained by fusing different components: siliceous or feldspathic sands and soda. It is used in the manufacture of glass and enamels. Reduced to powder and mixed with clay, frit is used in the preparation of soft-paste porcelain.

GLAZE Thin vitreous layer, transparent or coloured, applied to certain ceramics to render them impermeable. Glaze may contain lead (which should be very low solubility lead bisilicate) or tin. On the other hand it may contain neither. It is made with a base of feldspar, one of the components of porcelain.

*HAFT-RANGI* OR *MINAI* Seven-colour low-fired decoration, the firing takes place in an oxydising atmosphere.

HIGH FIRE Firing at high temperature. A high-fired decoration is done with colours capable of withstanding the firing temperature of the ceramic ware on which the design has been made. The colour range is restricted.

KAOLIN White argillaceous rock which is an essential constituent in the composition of hard-paste porcelain, giving it whiteness and plasticity. The word is derived from the Chinese *gaoling*, which is also the name of a site, Kao-Lin, not far from Jingdezhen (Fuliang district, Jiangxi province) from which this clay was extracted.

KHATAI The Khitan, who built an empire in northern China from 907 to 1122, originated the term that was used throughout Europe in the Middle Ages to denote China; it is still employed in Bulgaria and Russia in the form of Khitai.

KRAAK PORCELAIN Literally 'carrack porcelain', describing a consignment that owes its name to an incident when, in 1602, a Portuguese carrack was captured by the Dutch. The cargo consisted mainly of Chinese porcelain and was sold at auction in Amsterdam, fetching very high prices.

KUFIC Derived from the town of Kufa: angular characters of the first form of Islamic calligraphy employed for writing the Koran. From the tenth century, kufic script was replaced by a more flowing, supple and elegant style.

LEAD GLAZE Transparent glaze made of sand and lead sulphate or lead oxide (litharge). If tin oxide is added, it becomes white and opaque, as is the case with tin faiences. With the addition of certain metallic oxides capable of withstanding firing, it can be coloured. Used by the Chinese in the Han epoch, it was known in the Middle East from the second millennium BC.

LOW FIRE Firing at a moderate temperature of 900°C, making it possible to achieve a wide range of decoration,

MAIOLICA Originally the name of Hispano-Moresque ceramics exported from Spain to Italy. The term may be a corruption of Maiorca, from where the ships transporting this ware set sail. In Italy, majolica still signifies tin faience but elsewhere it is used solely for Italian faience pieces of the Renaissance.

OXIDES The colouring materials used for decorating ceramics develop and are fixed when exposed to heat. Only inorganic mineral substances can furnish the colorants capable of withstanding such temperatures, and these are the metallic oxides. The palette depends upon the temperature to which the oxides are subjected:
- Until the eighteenth century decoration was of the high-fire type and the oxides used were restricted to cobalt (blue), copper (green and red), manganese (brown-violet) and iron (brown, yellow, red).
- In the eighteenth century purples and pinks were introduced, thanks to the gold precipitate discovered by Cassius. But the palette was mainly expanded by the introduction of low-fire decoration.
- During the nineteenth century the following thirteen metals afforded an unlimited number of colours: antimony, chrome, cobalt, copper, gold, iridium, iron, manganese, nickel, platinum, silver, titanium, uranium.
- After the Second World War new colorants were discovered with a zircon base, very resistant to high temperatures. Around 1970, other derivatives of zirconium were found to withstand temperatures of 1350°C, these being the very stable, unalterable colours.

OXIDISING ATMOSPHERE, REDUCING ATMOSPHERE The atmosphere inside a kiln causes transformations in the course of firing; these vary according to the presence, to a greater or lesser degree, of oxygen. When the percentage of air is high, the firing is said to be oxidised, making it possible to obtain the classic colours. With a small percentage of air, the firing is said to be reduced. The low percentage of oxygen is due to the presence of reducing gases such as hydrogen, carbon monoxide, etc. The metallic oxides therefore assume different colours. This procedure is used in the manufacture of celadon (the colour of which is due to the iron oxide fired in a reducing atmosphere) and also to obtain metallic effects for lustred ceramics.

PETUNSE The term, derived from the Chinese *pai touen tsen*, or small black cubes, applies to a white feldspathic rock used in China for making porcelain.

PLATE For the sake of clarity, standard terms are used for the different parts of a plate: there are plates without wings in the form of a flattened bowl.

PORCELAIN Ceramic obtained from kaolin, feldspar and quartz, vitrified at a temperature of 1400–1500°C. The word, strangely, does not mean the same in China and in Europe. For the Chinese, porcelain is any ceramic piece fired at high temperature, which resonates when tapped. In the West, it is not only resonant but also pure white, translucent and impermeable. In some countries its properties are detailed and precisely established, including the degree of translucence, porosity and thickness.
The name 'porcelain' was given by Marco Polo because of the resemblance of this brilliant, transparent material to the highly prized shells of certain tropical ocean molluscs (Italian: *porcellana*, sea snail), which at this time were used as coins in Asia. In some languages of the Near East, in Greek and in Russian, the name has another

origin. The Chinese word *T'ien tseu* ('son of heaven'), in Persian *Bagh-pour* ('son of the goddess'), evolved into *Faghfour*. This title of the emperor of China was eventually applied to porcelain in a number of languages. True or hard-paste porcelain was produced in China during the T'ang dynasty of the eighth and ninth centuries. The secret of its manufacture was jealously guarded and it was rediscovered in the early eighteenth century in Saxony, spreading rapidly across Europe.

Research in various countries from the sixteenth century onward culminated in the discovery of artificial or soft-paste porcelain. This paste is formed from a mixture of white clay and frit which does not contain kaolin, the essential constituent of hard porcelain. Firing of these ceramics is effected at around 1000°C.

The paste of hard porcelain comprises 50 per cent kaolin, 25 per cent quartz – which serves as a binder and prevents deformation in the course of firing – and 25 per cent feldspar, which serves as the flux and causes transparency. These proportions vary to some extent in different areas of production.

PORCELAIN CABINET The curiosities cabinet appeared during the Renaissance. This was a piece of furniture with compartments and drawers, designed to accommodate rare and valuable objects of small dimensions. In the seventeenth century the range was narrowed and the cabinet came to be used specifically for collections of porcelain. During the eighteenth century no palace was considered complete without its porcelain cabinets, but they were conceived as being very different from a museum collection. What counted was not so much the quality and beauty of the porcelain ware, but its quantity. Viewed as a whole, the cabinet was intended to dazzle observers by its elaborate decoration and its collections.

The idea of these cabinets originated in Germany, where they were comparatively numerous, but other very famous examples were to be found in Spain, in Italy and at Brno in Moravia. These were not intended to accommodate collections of Chinese porcelain but to show off the products of national manufacturers. For example, the cabinet in the Doubsky palace of Brno was decorated by the Vienna factory: porcelain frames for paintings and mirrors, a porcelain chimney and porcelain slabs on doors, tables and chairs. A reconstruction of this cabinet is to be seen at the Museum of Decorative Arts in Vienna.

The most dedicated collector of porcelain was Augustus the Strong, elector of Saxony. In 1719 he inaugurated the construction of his porcelain cabinet, the Japanese palace, at Dresden, which was never completed.

SCALE Decorative motif formed of semicircles overlapping like fish scales. It is used for faience and porcelain.

SHARD A fragment or broken piece of pottery.

SLIP Clay combined with water used for joining together parts such as handles, feet and ornaments in relief. It can also be used for decorating porcelain and faience by trailing or pouring. Also important for slip-casting in plaster-of-Paris mould, objects of hollow-ware.

STONEWARE A very hard, compact and impermeable ceramic, and thus distinct from terracotta and faience. It is also opaque, which distinguishes it from porcelain. It is obtained from siliceous clay fired at a high temperature (1200–1300°C). The first examples of stoneware were produced in China during the Han period (206BC–AD220). In Europe it appeared in the fifteenth century.

TERRACOTTA Unglazed earthenware fashioned from clay and sand, dried and fired at 900–1000°C. It is porous and coloured, the colour being due to the metallic oxide that it contains. Usually the tone varies, according to the iron oxide content, from yellowish orange to brownish red. Any greyness indicates the presence of manganese oxide in the paste.

TIN GLAZE A white glaze, due to tin oxide, which is also opaque, so that the shard is not transparent.

VASE For purposes of clarification, the different parts of a vase are as shown on the opposite page.

VITRIFICATION Partial or total fusion of the components of the paste (stoneware or porcelain), which loses its porosity, becomes resonant and may even become translucent.

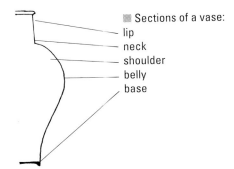

■ Sections of a vase:
lip
neck
shoulder
belly
base

■ Chinese vases: ideas for decoration

# Bibliography

Godden, G.A.
*Oriental Export Market Porcelain*
London, 1979. Granada


Medley, M.
*A Handbook of Chinese Art*
London, 1977. Bell & Hyman


Till, B. & Swart, P.
*Porcelain of the High Qing*
The Brian S. McElney Collection Exhibition Catalogue
Victoria BC, 1983. Art Gallery


Williams, C.A.S.
*Outlines of Chinese Symbolism and Art Motives*
New York, 1976. Dover Publications Inc.